# DEDICATION

My loving wife Jan who has stood by for over fourty four years and is
my inspiration and the true pioneer

My brother the Reverend Verne Wood, although totally paralyzed
with MS. Except for minual use of one hand has encouraged, guided
and edited the entire text.

# Building Our Dream in Remote Colorado

## Stephen Wood

iUniverse, Inc.
New York   Bloomington

# Building Our Dream in Remote Colorado

*The views expressed in this work are solely those of the author and do not necessarily reflect the views of the publisher, and the publisher hereby disclaims any responsibility for them.*

*iUniverse books may be ordered through booksellers or by contacting:*

*iUniverse*
*1663 Liberty Drive*
*Bloomington, IN 47403*
*www.iuniverse.com*
*1-800-Authors (1-800-288-4677)*

*Because of the dynamic nature of the Internet, any Web addresses or links contained in this book may have changed since publication and may no longer be valid.*

*ISBN: 978-1-4502-3396-5 (sc)*
*ISBN: 978-1-4502-3395-8 (dj)*
*ISBN: 978-1-4502-3424-5 (ebk)*

*Library of Congress Control Number: 2010907692*

*Printed in the United States of America*

*iUniverse rev. date: 7/8/2010*

# ** CHAPTER 1 **

In 1971 we purchased ten acres in a new development called Badger Creek Ranch. It is located approximately three hours southwest of Denver, Colorado where we were living at the time. The road leading into the property is two miles south of Hartsel, Colorado on Colorado Highway 9 and twenty one miles southwest to the development. At the time it was only graded and maintained for about eight miles the other thirteen miles was a ranch road and not a very good one at that.

We had been looking at property to buy and build on in the mountains west of Denver, Colorado for quite some time and had only found a few small acreages but they were way to expensive for our budget and to close to the city. I was raised on a farm in a very small rural area and was looking for something similar only in the mountains. When we answered an ad in the Rocky Mountain News of a development near Hartsel, Colorado with owner financing I felt this may be just what we had been looking for and made arrangements to meet the salesman.

We were met in Grant, Colorado on Highway 285 South by the Salesman who had a jeep, I did not think much of it at the time but after a two hour ride on Highway 285 South and another thirty minute ride on Highway 9 East to Hartsel, then turning on what he considered a road, my wife and I began to wonder if we had been kidnapped and taken to hell. Each time we confronted the salesman with our concerns we would always get the same stock answer, "we are almost there". I am happy to say we finally got there, not sure where and damn sure I could not find my way back but wherever "THERE" was, we were told we were here.

We were only the fourth or fifth to look at the new development. There was only one road to the development, we were told it was in phase one of three. There was a nicely laid out plate map to look at and red flags for the proposed roads and survey stakes for the property lines. After walking about what seemed twenty miles we decided on a ten acre site in the -Y- of two valleys.

The views were good and the land was mostly level. There were no trees on it, none even close, but it did have lots of cactus and stickers, one would think that at 9200 feet in elevation you would not have cactus and stickers but it did. It had two live streams on it, Badger Creek which ran approximately through the center and Cals Creek that angled across the southwest corner. Both creeks meet just a short distance down stream from our property line. Badger Creek is dry until just before the property line to the north where it emerges from the ground as a warm spring. I looked at my wife and said we can kill the stickers, we can plant trees but we can't make a stream and to have a good source of water on your property is priceless.

We sat in the jeep and made out the papers to purchase the land, lot four filing one. The ad in the paper we had answered had said owner financing and after filling out only one paper we were approved on the spot. It had no address because it had no access road yet just ten plus acres in the middle of a cow pasture. We agreed to pay three thousand two hundred dollars for our paradise and make payments of thirty two dollars a month till paid for. We did not know it or least realize it at the time but the developer of Badger Creek Ranch Company owned by Ken Barber of the Rawhide Realty Company in Colorado Springs, Colorado, is to this day one of the most honorable and honest men I have had the privilege to know. Not only did he agree to carry my note but the notes of most all others who bought here as well.

Mr. Barber was looking for property that he could develop, and along with other areas had also considered this particular twelve hundred acres as a possible site. The Freese Ranch had been purchased three years prior by a local rancher that owned the land adjacent to this parcel and was in no mood to sell. After several attempts Mr. Barber made an offer that Mr. McMurry, rancher/owner, couldn't refuse a decision that is regretted to this day by the family.

Being Mr. Barber's first attempt at developing he initiated some incentives that made his development more appealing and has stood the test of time. He had the foresight to zone it residential one (R-1) and wrote covenants that are still in effect with little change to this day governed by an elected vote of property owners. He also set aside a lot for county usage and gave the roads after there installation to the Park County Road and Bridge Department and a recreation area for all property owners complete with a fish pond and a very nice nature walk area. He drilled a public well complete with hand pump, still used by many property owners to this day. In its final stages the development consisted of two hundred eighty seven properties ranging in size from five to forty five acres all have county maintained roads to access their property. The roads are maintained by Park County Road and Bridge and are governed by Park County Building codes.

Badger Creek Ranch Development is located in the extreme southwest corner of Park County, Colorado, an area known as the upper Badger Basin of South Park. In the early days because of our location in the county and the remote accessibility, we were pretty much forgotten about and things pretty much got out of hand, the TV Series *South Park* has it pretty much nailed down as to life in the old days or even now days for that matter.

# **Chapter 2**

I was born and raised in northeastern Colorado in the sand hills, my father was a sharecropper and our farm had no electricity till my teen years. Being born and raised on a farm was the reason that made me want to get away from city life. As a child and through high school my brothers and I would start chores around 4:00 A.M. After milking the cows and separating the cream we did the chicken chores. Mom always had two hundred to four hundred chickens, some for butchering and most for laying then came the slopping of the hogs and feeding the calves.

Mom always had a big breakfast by 7:00 A.M. cooked on a wood stove utilizing corn cobs although I wasn't considered a big eater in our family my breakfast usually consisted of four eggs, seven to eight pancakes, sausage and milk.

We lived only about half a mile from our country school Amity now long gone. It was my brothers and my job to get there a half hour before school each day to haul water to the teacherage and schoolhouse. In the old days before school consolidation there were many small communities especially in the Midwest and West and most all had there own one room schools in the area. Most all of them taught first through eighth grade and had a house for the teacher and the family to live, built on the school property known as a teacherage. In the winter months we walked but most of the other kids rode horses or wagons and a few got driven or drove themselves.

At the time we had bought our acreage we were having a rough time of it. I had gotten a divorce from my first wife in 1965 and my wife had gotten a divorce from her husband in 1960. I had two sons from

4

my previous marriage and she had one son we had one boy together and another on the way yours, mine, and ours we were set on making it work and I really wanted my sons to know a rural life.

My wife Jan came from a small family one brother. Her dad had died shortly after her birth and her mother had remarried after the war but he passed away of an accident prior to our meeting. Jan had a rough childhood her mom and step dad had owned a laundry on West Colfax in Denver when not in school she would work in the laundry. In her teens she loved to roller skate and dance, she would walk from the laundry to the dance studio in downtown Denver or to the skating rink on East Colfax and Marion a distance of approximately five miles and then back home just so she could practice. At one time she performed at Elitch Gardens where there was a prestigious ballroom and theater.

Jan although not large in stature has a never quit attitude and a heart the size of a football field. While dating I took her to meet my parents I didn't know it at the time but Jan had never been on a trip out of Denver so for her to go to eastern Colorado, a one hundred and eighty mile journey, she saw it as an adventure. Unbeknown to me she had been preparing for over a week for our trip. I will never forget coming home from work to load our four door Olds Cutlass and finding a pile in the living room that looked like an itinerant farmer in the 1930's loading all of his belongings to escape a dust storm. I got quite a bit of it but had to leave some room for the four boys and us, after all we were only going for one night and two days.

After our marriage my mom took a shine to Jan and Jan to her. Jan became the daughter that Mom had never had and through that relationship Jan learned farm life, canning, gardening, butchering chickens, wheat and corn harvesting, along with chores and all the other amenities that goes with rural life. Mom was a home extension agent and belonged to many local clubs to which she introduced Jan. From that Jan learned quilting, cooking, crocheting, canning, freezing, and many other self sustaining talents. Jan loved it and became quite skilled and to this day is passing on her unique talents to anyone interested so when we bought our mountain paradise she had no qualms about leaving the city and living the rural life.

## ** Chapter 3 **

As with most all new property owners we could not wait to share our mountain retreat with friends and family. With pictures in hand we went home to my parents and spilled out all of our dreams.

After listening for two hours or so about our mountain paradise dad asked some thought provoking questions that only a father thinks of. Questions like what are you going to use for electric power? How are you going to get across the creek? If you build by the water, where do you put your septic system? How are you going to heat your new cabin? Where are the kids going to school? Will your car make it there and better yet make it back? Where is the closest store? Is it fenced? That is all open range you know, how deep is the well to get usable water and the cost of drilling it? How far to the nearest town that has jobs? If there are not good roads now, how are you going to get in, in the wintertime or better yet out? Are there any medical or emergency services available and if not how long before they reach you? What do you do for communication? Does the county plow your roads in the winter? Is there a fire department closer than a hundred miles? After two to three hours of grilling and exposed to more reality than one should be exposed in a lifetime, I was not nearly as proud of our mountain retreat as when we first got there and my wife was ready to call in the contract.

Our trip home that weekend proved to be a turning point in our lives. Dad's reality check had given us plenty to think about but had also created a challenge on just how we were going to make it work. Jan set about a plan in stages and budgets and I set about where to start. I felt priority number one would be a place to stay while we were up there.

Jan and I had purchased a sixteen foot camp trailer two years earlier so felt quite comfortable in using it while building. I had asked dad for his advice on many of the issues he had raised. Having remodeled a farmhouse that had been built out of a barn along with most all machinery that he had either built or redesigned, I figured he would be my best source of information. Among the things we discussed was how to build a septic system knowing that this would have to be one of the first things done. In late 1971 I had arranged to get four days off by that time we had been able to get a septic tank and the piping that Dad had designed and laid out along with picks and shovels and lots of supplies.

Mom and dad had come up the afternoon before we were to leave so we could get an early start to the Promised Land the next morning. With dad's pickup and my old '59' Dodge, four kids and two dogs we started our adventure. With a refrigerator box I had acquired, I had made a camper in the back of my pickup. I put some plastic over a hole made for a window on each end, made a door in one side, gave the boys some colors and coloring books and told them to decorate the camper on our way up. We loaded the tank on Dad's pickup and filled it with groceries, water, tools, blankets, you name it we took it and filled the rest of my pickup with stuff we just could not leave without.

It was cloudy in Denver but not too cold the shortest distance to our property was highway 285 from Denver through Turkey Creek Canyon to Bailey, Colorado through South Park and Fairplay. We had stopped in Bailey for gas as the only other town between Bailey and our property with a gas station was Fairplay and the gas there was always much higher. We felt the chill in the air at Bailey but figured after all we were in the mountains. All was going well after leaving Bailey, we had given the boys some snacks and the decorating was going fine in the camper.

Halfway up Kenosha Pass it started to snow, by the time that we topped out at 10,000 plus feet we were in a heavy mountain snow. Dad was following me but my wipers were leaving streaks on the windshield and I was having a hard time seeing the road, I stopped and ask Dad to lead. Jefferson, Colorado is located at the bottom of Kenosha Pass a distance of about six miles by the time we had gotten there the snow had let up but the wind was blowing pretty hard creating a ground blizzard.

You could not see the road or ditches but could see the tops of the linear posts and the tops of the fence posts on either side. We asked the people at the Jefferson store the only store in town if the road was open. In good and understandable South Park Lingo we were told if you drive it and make it, it is open, if not it is closed. It was open.

We left Fairplay south on highway 285 by the time we had only gone a few miles the snow had stopped the wind had greatly subsided and the sun was out but we had been on the road seven hours and it was getting late. The kids had every blanket we owned and being made of cardboard and wet their camper was collapsing around them. They said they were okay and having fun and to just keep going, we put the youngest in front with us and left the three oldest to fend for them selves and once again headed for the Promised Land. We made it at last light and our camper looked like the Taj Mahal. By the next morning Taj Mahal had lost a lot of its luster what with two dogs, four kids, and four adults in a sixteen foot camper with only two fold out beds it just had not made for a good night's rest.

Badger Creek at that time was two inches wide and quarter inch deep it ran through a ravine with approximately seven foot high walls on each side straight up and down and about forty foot wide at its narrowest point. I used a pick and shovel to cut in steps on the east side of the bank to get down to the water, I then dug a hole in the stream bed and put an old mop bucket we had brought with us in the hole, it filled rather quickly and I was able to fill water containers for our needs we even drank it thus the beginning of our water supply.

Dad and I had laid out the area that he thought would make a nice cabin spot and measured and flagged it for the septic system. I had always wanted a cabin close to a pond so I could fish from the deck, Dad being an avid outdoorsman and fisherman agreed to that plan one of the few things we found in common on that trip. With pick and shovel in hand we began to dig a hole for our septic tank. There is a good reason they call it the Rocky Mountains, we knew right away we were not in the eastern Colorado sand hills any more. The fiberglass septic tank was ten foot long five foot high and four feet wide and the hole needed to be dug approximately seven foot deep that's a big hole and that is not counting the sixty feet of leach line and thirty feet of lead line. By lunchtime we had pretty much decided that we needed a backhoe tractor or at least a Caterpillar dozer.

The contractor that was building the roads, Hutcheson Excavating, was in the area as we could hear their equipment on occasion and had seen some vehicles on the new road approximately eight hundred yards west and above our lot so we knew we were not alone. Dad suggested that we find them and get a price for digging our septic, not a bad idea as I had already gone through my one pair of gloves and was on my second set of blisters.

After lunch we all piled into dad's pickup mom, dad and the youngest in the front Jan, three older boys and myself in the back. It was cloudy and windy and good chill in the air but not snowing, thank God for Mom and Jan, it seems they were the only ones with half a brain as they insisted that we take some comforters. They were the homemade kind made at quilting bees and made from old farm jeans and overalls and filled with batting in the middle. They weighed a ton, but kept you warm on very cold nights or in the back of a pickup truck at 9200 feet in the rocky mountains in late fall.

Our only access was from the proposed road on the east side and there was no way to get across Badger Creek to the west side. Dad and I had decided the cabin should be on the west side of the creek this presented another problem how do you cross a streambed that is forty feet wide with seven foot banks on either side to get to the other side? We drove across the cow pasture road from our property to the newly made road. They had put in two large culverts each four foot high to get across Badger Creek and made a cut up the side of the hill it was only about the width of a dozer blade.

When we got on the new road it was pretty soft but had tire tracks where vehicles had been going but without a four wheel drive vehicle we only made it about half way up the hill. We had no more than began to ponder our situation when a pickup truck came down the hill slid to a stop in front of us and had the audacity to ask what we were doing here and with only a two wheel drive truck. We introduced ourselves and pointed to our camper with the explanation that we had purchased lot four filing one and were going to find the contractor that was putting in these so called roads in which we were stuck in the middle.

Needless to say my smart reply could only be made to Mr. Hutcheson owner and so-called road builder, not a good start to a relationship especially in South Park, Colorado. I guess he could tell a hayseed when he saw one as he mellowed down a bit and I apologized, he backed up a little threw us a chain and with him in reverse and us going forward pulled us up to the top of the hill. We explained our needs and he agreed to come out the next day and take a look but was making a repair run for one of the pieces of his equipment at that time.

We got down the hill and back down to the camper. Dad and I were wet and covered with mud but thanks to the girls everyone else was warm and dry. I guess that was my first bath in paradise and Dad's as well. We stripped down to our BVDs at the creek bottom just down stream from my mop bucket water well and proceeded to bathe, it only took about five minutes and Dad was blue and I had lost most feeling on all parts of my body. The rest of the afternoon was spent around a good campfire wrapped inside our comforters.

We had a good wood source, about three hundred yards up the hill on the west side of the creek there had been a large holding corral there but was pretty much dilapidated so we all pulled down logs from it and got them across the ravine to our fire ring. For those not familiar with the term holding corral it's an area where ranchers would drive their cattle into for branding, sorting or to load or drive them to another destination. I guess that also was a first, the first campfire and the first lumber on our property.

Mr. Hutcheson was there early the next morning and after looking at our plans he agreed with dad that we needed to build on the west side of the creek as it was higher ground and would support our septic system he also came to the conclusion that we needed to build a dam or fill to cross the ravine. To get the material needed he would cup out the east and west side of the banks, it would also make a nice pond.

He had a backhoe he was using to put in culverts on the new roads and agreed to dig the necessary hole and trenches for our septic. After getting excited about the prospect of actually seeing progress came the reality that it was not free. He said that if I did not need it right away he would work it in when he built our access road and the cost would be approximately one hundred and fifty dollars plus permit fees by today's standards that is not even a good meal out but it sounded like a million dollars to Jan and I. I was honest and told him I did not have the money to pay him now so he made arrangements to make payments Jan and I were overwhelmed by his trust and honesty. I was beginning to feel with people like Mr. Hutcheson we could really make this our home some day.

# **Chapter 4**

Mr. Hutcheson in our visiting had also given us an insight on the area we were beginning to love. He had pointed to an old hay buck to the west and up Cals Creek valley still there to this day. A hay buck is a triangular shaped device mounted on long logs on the bottom so it can be pulled and stands about twelve foot high with a long log suspended by chain a little off center from the top with a pull cable on one end and a grapple hook on the other and was used in the early days to lift bundled hay into stacks that when completed looked like huge loaves of bread from a distance. It kept the hay from spoiling and could then be used for animal feed in the winter. He explained if we took the cow road in front of our property and went north about a half mile we would go through Badger Creek. The term Cow Road, also called Ranch Roads comes from ranchers or farmers that in order to access their property drove across land in no orderly fashion and are full of curves, washes to cross, around or straight up hills and consists of two wagon or tire tracks that made it easy for cattle to follow, they were usually badly washed and rutted. It was dry where the road went through the ravine but was pretty steep on both sides so we would need to go through it at a good speed and not stop. He told us that if we would go to the hilltop and take a left we would go past an old holding pen, we knew where that was it was our wood source but did not tell him as maybe we should have not been using the logs. He told us to just follow the road past the hay buck through Cals Creek and stay on the Cow Road and in about fourteen miles we would be at highway 285, we should take a left on highway 285 and would only be about six miles from Buena Vista, Colorado.

Buena Vista is a town with a population of about one thousand two hundred it had two grocery stores, schools, etc. I asked about jobs and was told that although the pay was far from Front Range standards there were quite a few jobs available although most were seasonal.

When we left for Buena Vista it was still morning, we took Dad's truck three in front, five in back. It was mostly cloudy but some blue sky here and there it wasn't real cold probably in the thirties. We had not gone more than two miles from our property when we found ourselves in some of the most beautiful country one can only imagine. There is a beautiful forest of Ponderosa pine, Blue Spruce, Engleman spruce, and large areas of Aspen. The leaves had long dropped but the forest floor was covered leaving one only to imagine the magnificence of summer and fall.

As we drove we found the road to be at least as good as the road in from Hartsel and only twelve or so miles to the highway instead of twenty one miles on the Hartsel road. We went down a hill into a bottom area it looked pretty boggy and the tire tracks seemed to be pretty deep in the saw grass, a heavy thick grass and only grows in or near water. Dad and I got out and walked it; there were a few beaver ponds to the left and a small running creek that we had to cross. The road seemed to go to the right up a pretty steep hill but we felt we could make it if we gave it hell and did not let up.

We all got our positions in the truck and away we went through the saw grass marsh across the stream and up the hill, we had no problem although there were a few times I am sure the pickup was airborne. When we topped out at a place known as the Black Dumps we stopped the truck and could only stare at the panoramic view in front of us, to this day I always slow down at that point and on many occasions stop just to see God's hand at work. The ridge known as the Black Dumps is named because in the early twenties two miners found a coal outcropping there but the coal was of poor quality and petered out but had left three or four piles of black dirt.

You overlook Bassam Park, an open park with few trees and rolling hills rising west to a tree lined ridge and in the background part of the Sangre De Cristo and all of the Collegiate range. The Collegiate range consists of the most Fourteener peaks (peaks with elevations of 14,000+ feet) in Colorado. To your left is Aspen Ridge it is known as the largest continuous Aspen grove in the world. If you are not spiritual before you arrive there you will be after viewing this site, I did not know the ranges or the park names then only the inspiring beauty.

*View from the Black Dumps*

We continued our journey into town, the further we drove the more beauty we encountered. Through Columbine Gulch with several beaver ponds along our route and beautiful Aspen groves mixed with conifers into a wonder of the world. As we came out of Columbine Gulch we went up a short but steep hill to encounter a large rock out cropping jutting up to what seemed to heaven with beaver ponds and a stream curving around its base. As we rounded the corner there were other out cropping all separate and rising out of the valley floor to a height not known  they were almost flat on their tops, this area is known as the Castles. We went through Trout Creek and took a left on highway 285.

I am going to inject a history of the Castles although not known to us at that time they are on many and most all maps and historic ledgers.

Going south on highway 285 from the top of Trout Creek pass you will enter Trout Creek Canyon, at that point is where Chafee County Road 307 intersects. The geology is dramatic as these remnants are a part of an immense pyroclastic lava flow from an explosive volcanic eruption southwest of Buena Vista some 36 million years ago, an exposure of the great conformity attracts geologists from all over the world. It is here that 1.7 billion year old pre Cambrian granites meet much younger Paleozoic sedimentary rocks, there appears to be a billion year gap in the geologic record. The Ute Indians came to this area for flint, wild game, and Pinion nuts, and followed Trout Creek up to the South Park hunting grounds, even today hikers find fashioned arrowheads and flint chips.

*The Castles*

When we arrived in Buena Vista we were impressed with the town a real mountain town, and the people seemed friendly. We got a few groceries and some ice a real treat we had packed sandwiches for lunch and found a nice park with tables ate our lunch and just enjoyed the town.

We left for our property around 2:00 P.M. but missed our turnoff, after only a mile or so knew we had not seen the sights before so turned around and found our cutoff had we been looking there was a sign that indicated Bassam Park and Aspen Ridge but not knowing where we had been that didn't mean much, now we know.

The reverse trip was just as beautiful only in reverse, when you get to the Black Dumps going east you see Black Mountain in the distance and a good portion of the upper Badger Basin. When we crossed the bog we did not go quite as fast partly because it is downhill and secondly we felt a little more confident. We got back to our paradise about 3:30 P.M. and started a nice campfire ate supper and roasted marshmallows and visited well into the night.

We had made some adjustments in our sleeping arrangements by the second night. The two older boys and dogs slept in the camper box, which made room for the rest of us in the camper still crowded but more comfortable sleeping. We left for our home in Denver the next morning thus ending our adventure in "Cactus Acres" which Jan had dubbed it only after our visit when we took the camper there. She had spent the next four or five days getting the stickers out of the dogs, it was not my first choice of names but by then reality had taken precedence.

# **Chapter 5 **

I had only three jobs since high school, my first was working on a sheep ranch in Colorado and I lasted only about nine months and found out why there had been cattle and sheep wars in the early days of the west, cattle don't stink and aren't nearly as dumb.

I moved to Denver to find fame and fortune only to find a job delivering soda and driving in traffic all day. Most people were okay in a city sort of way but after a year or so I fit right in and kept selling soda. At the time I was getting paid more money than I thought was in the world. The trouble was it took it all just to pay rent, food, gas, and fun, the fun things taking most.

My third job was working for a truck line I was told I had to join a union. I did not know much about unions but when I found out I could start for one dollar and eighty nine cents an hour with health and insurance benefits I fell in love with them. With the added income we felt we could work on our property the next summer.

We bought our first home in 1971 in Denver, it was a fixer upper and the bank used our remodel as our down payment. I was always good at building, being raised on a farm if you wanted it you built it, bent it, or welded it, so I rebuilt it. We had to borrow money to get carpet, cabinets, paint, etc., but we got our home. Jan had also taken a job so the winter of 71-72, was spent working to pay off those bills and the earthwork at our paradise.

In early spring of 72 we headed back up to the Promised Land. Due to the bad weather in the fall we had never gotten back up to Cactus Acres so we were very excited about the trip. We were really anxious to see our new pond and dam along with the work on the septic. My youngest son was born April 1972 and was almost four weeks old so we figured he was old enough to make our weekend trip.

It seems I always loaded the pickup to the max when going to the property this trip was no exception. We decided to go in the short way, actually it is a mile further than the Hartsel way but this being our second trip in on this route we were not aware of this, we left the highway at the Castles and headed in.

The Front Range weather channels really never include our property area and still don't once you leave Bailey or Fairplay you are pretty much on your own. We have learned over the years that in two miles the weather can change dramatically, it can be sunny in Buena Vista, Hartsel or even at the Black Dumps but have a foot or so of snow at our property or vice versa, such was the case on this trip.

By the time we had gotten the nine miles to the Black Dumps we were in about a foot of blowing snow with a two wheel drive truck and a four week old baby.

It is pretty flat on top and the snow had pretty much blown off and there was a good place to turn around. At that time there was a fence with a gate to go through now there is a cattle guard and gate. It is the county line between Chaffee and Park Counties. The gate was open but had about a two foot drift through it the drift was only about twenty feet wide with open ground on both sides. I pondered taking a run at it but I got some good advice from Jan reminding me of our new son and the fact we had no chains for our truck and no shovel, she was right of course I had about everything else but chains or a shovel.

She also mentioned the bog at the bottom of the steep hill, I really wanted to go to our property so decided to walk down the hill to see what the snow was like through the bog. I did not have to walk very far, for just over the brink of the hill I found where the snow that had blown off the top of the hill had landed. Not only could I not see the road but also the Aspen trees on both sides were partially buried this pretty much dictated my decision to turn around and go home but before we left I decided to unload my treasures and get them on my next trip in. I had bought up some old lumber that I had scavenged from the truck docks, pallets, metal strapping, nails, and other building supplies I unloaded it next to the fence and headed home.

As with other trips we were learning a lot about our area, on the way home we stopped in Fairplay and had breakfast a real treat for us and the boys as we rarely ate out. We met an old timer setting at the table next to us and in good farmer fashion started a conversation. He informed us that the road in from the Castles was a forest access road and mostly used during the summer by ranchers in our area and hunters in the fall he also gave us a little history of the area. He could not believe they were developing that area known as the Freese Ranch. Around the 1870's to the 1920's it was a thriving area with a store, school, and church and had a population between two hundred fifty to four hundred people. There was a stagecoach line that ran from Salida, Colorado to Fairplay and around 1887 there were two railroads, one ran in to Chubb Park an area about eight miles to the southeast of our subdivision and one through Trout Creek Canyon. The Colorado Midland railroad connected Colorado Springs to Newcastle, Colorado on the western slope until around 1918. The line hauled freight to Leadville, moved coal from the Newcastle mine, limestone from Newitts quarry and transported passengers to Glenwood Springs.

George Leon Hardy an early Chaffee County Commissioner built the Leon Hardy cutoff in 1872, it ran from Chubb Park to the farmlands along the Arkansas River north of Buena Vista this toll road and mail route was also a shortcut to the Leadville mines. Arnold Gulch provided access to Traid Ridge and Bald Mountain silver mines, active ore producers until the 1893 silver crash. Arkansas valley ranching families drove their cattle up the gulch to Bassam, Herring and Chubb Parks every spring.

The stage line serviced the now ghost town of Turret, which also had a rail spur from Salida. From Turrent the stage line went over Cameron Pass to the now ghost town of Whitehorn and several large quarries as well as the Golden Wonder Mine, the Gold Bug Mine and several others. From Whitehorn there were quite a few ranches and mines, it continued through Herring Park to the Freese store and on to Hartsel, Garo and Fairplay. We were told of a large cave that was known to be the highest dry cave in the U.S. and had been explored by the Denver Museum of Natural History where camel, saber tooth tiger fossils had been exhumed along with seahorses, shells and other prehistoric life but is on private land and has since been closed to all.

He had presented quite a history lesson but not only did we not remember many of the names of the towns, mines or railroads but also didn't have a clue where any of those places were. On our trip home we discussed our history lesson and got a real sense that we were in a part of what had been an important and wild part of Colorado.

# **Chapter 6**

After that trip we decided to wait until June or July to try again it was during that time when I designed our first off grid electric system. I will use the term "OFF GRID" and "ON GRID" many times in my text and feel they need to be explained. The term ON GRID means that your electricity comes from a commercial source that you must rely on. OFF GRID means that there is no commercial electric source available, as in our case the closest source of electric power being over twelve miles away and relying on your own production for all your electricity needs. I knew as a youngster on the farm how we had managed so with this small amount of knowledge and some research I decided that to build a cabin off grid was to just wire and plumb it like a big camper trailer.

Back then there was not much about solar, wind, inverters and such although wind chargers had been in existence since before the 1900's on farms and ranches throughout the Midwest mostly 24 volt systems and not very reliable. The old Delco systems powered by a hit and miss engine. "An old type engine that only fired every other revolution and was used mostly for industrial applications". It used kerosene mixed with water the smaller engines would run about eight hours on one gallon of fuel. It was not a good choice not only because of its design but also because of our altitude and temperature ranges.

I had written the Chamber of Commerce in Buena Vista, Hartsel and Fairplay but only Fairplay returned any information. The closest county school would be a forty five mile ride one way we would have to drive the kids the first twenty six miles to Hartsel because there would be no bus service and very little maintenance in the winter. Along with a list of other things I found it was not unusual for winter temps to go below -50 and -10 to -20 degrees was pretty much the norm through January and February. With this wealth of information and studying the water and electric systems of RV's I set about how to make everything work.

The first thing I needed was a new generator, for those not familiar with this term a generator in this usage is an electrical device powered by a small engine capable of putting out a continuous sixty cycle alternating current (ac) like that used in your home but portable so it can be used in remote areas where on grid electricity is not available. There are quite a few companies that build these but generators of this type are somewhat expensive. They come in different power ranges but the 5000 to 7000 watt units seems to be the most popular and would power most household appliances.

The power output is rated at sea level and the higher the altitude the less the output. At our altitude of 9200 feet there is approximately a 33% loss of factory output, that is to say that a 5000watt generator at our altitude is actually capable of producing only about 3700 watts. I was told at my work place to check out army surplus stores as during the war the big guns on ships were powered by using generators.

With little more knowledge than a first grader learning about girls I figured this was just the ticket. The trouble was they were wired 24volt direct current (dc) for the turrets, a device that rotated the guns aiming system. It would take a master electrician with World War II canon experience to convert it to usable ac power.

They were inexpensive most ran from about seventy five dollars to one hundred fifty dollars, but they weighed about a half ton not my idea of portable. I know I ran a little off track but with a very limited budget and a family to raise that was a lot of money. Our house payment was one hundred thirty nine dollars a month and that came hard every month so when I found a new portable generator a 5500 watt Ag Tech for five hundred dollars it seemed like a fortune but if we were to build and eventually live on Cactus Acres we were going to need one.

We hadn't seen the excavation work at our property but through the winter Jan had managed to get it paid for and was two payments ahead on our property. It probably had a lot to do with eating a lot of spaghetti and chicken, being this affluent we arranged to buy the Ag Tech Generator.

Like most men when I bought it I knew it was the best money could buy and felt I had gotten a really good deal. It was powered by a ten horse power Briggs and Stratton engine and weighed about one hundred twenty pounds certainly much more portable. For another one hundred and fifty dollars I could have gotten it with an electric start but by now you know that was more than another house payment and completely out of the question. It took two men and a boy to pull the rope starter when cold, a problem that cost Jan a lot of lonely nights we will get to that story later.

# ** Chapter 7 **

By June I was a mess and just had to get to Cactus Acres. Since our last attempted trip I had been collecting old shipping crates from around Denver. I would spot them while making deliveries and asked if I could have them they were more than happy to get rid of them since it saved them a trip to the dump. I would go back after work, tear them down and remove all the nails from the lumber. I kept most of the nails after all they too were reusable and took the lumber home.

Our Denver home was beginning to look more like a lumberyard than a house and the neighbors were getting a little upset, in June the decision was made to go to Cactus Acres. I borrowed a trailer from a friend, loaded my 1959 Dodge pickup and hooked up the trailer. The trailer was made out of an old four foot by eight foot pickup bed the tires were pretty good and built on the old frame I figured I could haul a pretty good load with it.

I knew from my trucking experience that the legal height on a highway was twelve foot six inches and you could legally load up to four foot longer than the trailer length without lights or flags. I started loading that Thursday after work and finished the following Friday after work I had it tied down very securely. No, I did not go the legal height as all I had was a six foot step ladder but I did get it about ten foot high and decided that was about all the trailer could handle anyway. I did use the extra four feet making it twelve foot long. I gave no thought to my poor old thirteen year old truck with about a million miles on it.

We left for paradise Saturday morning around 4:00 A.M. I had pulled the load one or two miles as a test to see how it would handle. It pulled hard up a little hill by our home, so decided to take Interstate

25 south to Colorado Springs then Highway 24 to Hartsel. I had never taken that route to Cactus Acres and it was about forty miles further but only had one pass on it. Wilkerson pass is only around 10,000ft at the summit. Highway 285 to Fairplay on the other hand seems to go uphill from Denver to the top of Kenosha Pass. I really don't know how I figured this was the best route as Denver is 5400ft in elevation and Cactus Acres is 9200ft, either way I had to go up 3800ft.

We headed out five boys, two dogs, Jan and my self, we had the baby in front with us and the four older boys and two dogs in the back. The boys were in a new camper box, this one a bigger refrigerator box and I had added two windows, one so they could see into our cab and the other to see to the rear.

Things went pretty well until Monument Hill south of Castle Rock, Colorado. It pulled hard but I was pulling the hills in second gear. My 59 Dodge had a 318 cubic- inch engine and a three-speed column shift, by today's standards that is not much come to think of it that was not much by 1972 standards either but I was proud of it and that was what I had.

By the time I had topped out on Monument I was in low gear doing about five M.P.H. and the old Dodge was getting pretty hot. I got to a pull out and let the boys out to get rid of some built up energy while it cooled. Going south up Monument Hill is about a five mile incline although I had been that way to Colorado Springs a few times I hadn't realized how long an upgrade it was. In a car going sixty or seventy M.P.H. you get a much different prospective than you do from an old pickup pulling a somewhat overloaded trailer.

The downhill side is a straight road with a 7% grade that is pretty steep for those not familiar. At the bottom is a weigh station where trucks are stopped and checked for weight and legal documents, they also have to pay a Colorado State road tax. There are usually one or two State Patrol cars there and this day was no exception. The station has a clear view from the top of Monument Hill to the bottom.

When we started down the hill and being a truck driver I put my truck in low gear so I could use the engine to hold back the load and only pump the brakes to keep a slow but steady decent. Half way down my old Dodge got real tired and slipped out of gear. If you are a trucker or have ever had that experience God help you. I immediately put on the emergency brake and started pumping the brakes to get stopped. When it comes out of gear going downhill pulling a heavy load a lot of things can go wrong in a hurry. Number one when it comes out of gear the engine speed revs up to about mach one making it impossible to get the vehicle back into any gear. Secondly your brakes get hot almost instantly making them slick, losing their grip, rendering them useless, and the weight of the loaded trailer pushes your vehicle, this is usually the time where you grab your bottom and bend over and kiss it goodbye, I didn't have time to use this tactic I just rode it down.

My real clue on how bad our situation was when I looked out my side window and saw the trailer still hitched to the truck trying to pass me sideways. I don't recall the screaming, but found out later that Jan was so hoarse she could only whisper. When I finally got my old Dodge into high gear I released all the brakes and stepped on the gas thus straightening out our rig.

The pull off into the weigh station is long and straight as is the exit. I don't know how fast I went through the station but I do remember seeing two or three truckers that did the ten-yard dash in two seconds. I got it stopped just before reaching the Interstate and I am proud to say I never lost a board off the load. The Highway Patrol was not so impressed they were there before I got stopped, although totally impressed with my driving ability they made me take it to an empty part of the lot and park it. It is amazing that ability and utter fear was used in the same sentence but that seemed to be the case.

After about an hour's lecture on thirty to forty violations, most of which could have gotten me some pokey time, all of which could have cost me my driver's license that if revoked would have cost me my job, they decided that if I would unload about two thirds of my load and get my brakes checked as soon as possible they would not sight me. I don't know why they didn't, maybe it was because of the pale look still on my wife's face or the baby crying or the kids in back with a death stare on their faces or maybe the fresh smell of sewage coming from all of us, anyway I thanked them and agreed to all of their demands.

After unloading my prized lumber in a remote area of the weigh station, we once again set out for the Promised Land. We did not encounter any more problems but found highway 24 west of Manitou Springs, to Divide, Colorado a distance of twenty five to twenty six miles and with few exceptions not a downhill on it. From the bottom of Wilkerson Pass to the summit is a steady incline for about eight miles, so I am not sure with my original load my old Dodge would have made it anyway.

It was middle afternoon by the time we had gotten things unloaded and Jan had opened up the camp trailer. The pond was beautiful about a half-acre in size, but the top of the dam was barely wide enough to drive across. When we agreed to have it built nothing was said about a discharge culvert through or under the dam. Mr. Hutcheson had made a low cut out on the west side to let the water flow out. The trouble was that even with just a small stream it had already began to wash out the backside of the dam. Knowing that I am not the shiniest apple in the tree I was intelligent enough to know something had made that deep ravine as far as I could see in any direction and there must have been a reason for the two very large culverts for the main road to pass over the creek, as it was this dam wasn't going to last.

The hole and trenches for the septic was pretty much dug as laid out and he had even lowered the tank in place for us a job I had given considerable thought to but had not a found a good solution, therefore I was greatly relieved when this was done for us. I went about putting in the leach line that same evening and well into the night. When you only have two days a week and have to travel this far sleep becomes secondary.

I had the leach line in and leveled to grade and was starting the inlet line when Mr. Hutcheson stopped by. After some coffee and good visiting he said if I wanted he would come over when in our area again and back fill it. He also informed us of three other families building up here and I should meet them, I felt good knowing I was not the only idiot on the planet. In our conversation he had told me I needed to get a culvert through the dam and if possible to concrete the spillway to keep it from washing, he said we had been extremely fortunate to have had a very mild winter and that the snow melt had been slow and that was probably what saved the dam.

We left for Denver in the late afternoon taking highway 285 north, I felt good knowing that the next time up we could use our septic system but knew my time was limited on the dam.

# **Chapter 8**

Our next trip was three weeks later at the end of June I had gotten my new generator and a lot more lumber. I had gone back to the weigh station the next Saturday after our mishap only to find all the lumber I had unloaded there gone. I was angry and happy at the same time, angry because of all the work I had gone through to get it and happy knowing I actually had something good enough for someone else to want.

My Dad had gone to an estate auction and brought a pretty new sixty foot by ten foot mobile home, that was a shock and we didn't have the money for it. He had bought it at a very reasonable price and it came with all the furniture, Dad said we could pay him as we got the money. I knew they did not have the money to spend and we had just accumulated another bill, it seems I was getting my priorities all mixed up but it sure would be a good place for all of us to cook and sleep while building at Cactus Acres.

The next trip was to fix the dam and try to make it flood proof, to do that I needed a culvert. I had seen tubing at an army surplus store while looking at generators so decided to start there. It turned out the tubing I had seen were empty shell casings from some kind of guns on a navy ship, they were eight inches in diameter and three foot long and after lying them out I figured I could connect them to make a fine culvert, they were only one dollar each. I bought enough to make a twenty-four foot long culvert they would be easy to haul and did I mention they were only one dollar each?

That weekend I loaded the pickup camper and the borrowed trailer closer to legal limits and by 4:00 A.M. Saturday morning we were on our way. This time we followed highway 285 through Fairplay, all went well except going up Red Hill Pass a short but steep pass just north of Fairplay. I seemed to lose power as soon as I topped out but going down and across South Park it ran fine.

We went in on the forest road we now knew by Road number 187 at the Black Dumps all the lumber, strapping, etc. I had unloaded in the snow was gone this seemed to be becoming a habit. The bog was dry but you could see where someone had really been stuck at an earlier time, it made me think that in any rain or inclement weather maybe I should seriously consider an alternative route.

On the trip up, Jan and I had discussed where we were going to put the trailer house so we could hook it to our sewer but still not interfere with our building. After getting the camper opened up and the boys a snack we tied up the dogs, we were getting smarter especially after the sticker escapade. Jan took the boys across the dam and started measuring and laying out a site for the camper. I had brought up four sacks of concrete mix but needed sand we had plenty of water a wagon, wheelbarrow and buckets, along with my usual lumber load.

When we had taken our trip to Buena Vista we had gone through Badger Creek just north of our property. I had seen a lot of sand and rock in the wash sure enough when I took a closer look it had excellent sand and rock mix and no dirt, much better than anything available in Eastern Colorado. With the gravel loaded in the back of the truck, cement, and water I proceeded to make my concrete spillway. After blisters on both hands and every finger and a back that felt like I had carried the trailer house over the dam I had it pretty much finished, but it had taken me well into the evening.

The boys lived for their campfires as did Jan and I and it gave us a good opportunity to visit. It was during one of our more serious conversations that Jan asked how we were going to get the camper over the dam better yet, how were we going to get the sixty foot long trailer house over? There she goes again asking logical questions about problems I had not yet considered. I knew the top of the dam was way to narrow and probably too soft to pull the camper trailer across, I could barely make it with the truck and there was no way to get our new mobile home across.

But first things first I still had to put a culvert through the dam. Digging a trench across the dam could be done all right but the culvert needed to be lower than the spillway. If I dug my trench deep enough to put the culvert where it belonged, the water in the pond would wash out my trench and would probably wash out the whole dam. After some good old-fashioned pondering and sleeping on it that night, I came up with the solution. I would start the trench on the waterside of the dam and dig it eight inches below the water line but only about four foot long. I would add my section of culvert and start back filling it as I went thus forcing the water through the culvert but holding back the water. I put the culvert on the opposite side of the spillway I have no idea why.

By Sunday noon I was making like a human mole. My plan was working fine and because it was a fresh fill and always having the trench full of water the digging wasn't bad but very muddy. It was only about fourteen foot through the dam at that level which gave me enough pipe left over to overhang the discharge far enough out to not wash the backside of the dam. I had also extended a three-foot section on the inlet so the water would not vortex or back wash. I was feeling pretty clever by now as it actually worked.

Jan and the boys had spent most of their two days picking up rocks and hauling with the wagon and wheelbarrow to the dam and placing them on the banks, by the time Sunday afternoon came our place was really starting to take shape. We were late starting home and Jan the boys and I were pretty much done in.

On the way home I don't think we had gone two miles before the boys had gone to sleep in their camper box. We had gone through Fairplay and Jefferson on highway 285 and were starting up Kenosha Pass when I felt a bad vibration and heard a loud knocking in the engine. As a boy on the farm, one of our biggest past times was building sand buggies out of old pickups and cars to chase coyotes. Most of these vehicles did not last long before we would blow up an engine or roll them so I knew instantly what had happened.

I had to make a fast decision either stop and try to get a ride home or keep going and try to make the top of Kenosha Pass where I knew I could coast probably all the way to Grant where there was a phone. This was way before cell phones (info for the younger generation) I slowed up and put the old Dodge in low and headed for the top. Usually, unless a connecting rod breaks and goes through the engine block, if you just idle the engine it will keep running, it makes a hell of noise but runs.

As a youth we once blew a rod on an old Olds straight eight engine about twenty miles from the farm and made it home. Remembering that coyote hunt and knowing the engine was probably toast anyway I had nothing to lose.

When we topped out I got to a turn out where I knew I could push it and get it going downhill. I didn't see any oil on the engine or the ground and when I checked the oil it was fine. I started it up and headed down the hill. By keeping the clutch in, the engine just idled and I used the breaks to hold it back. I figured if it got away from me all I had to do was let out the clutch. I was sure if that happened it would lock up the engine but we would stop.

At Grant we were doing pretty well at fifteen to twenty M.P.H. we stopped and called my brother in Denver. He said he would head out and watch for us so off we went. Knowing help was on the way it gave me a good feeling so with this attitude I wanted to see just how far it would go.

Grant to Bailey is about ten to twelve miles and not many uphill areas, mostly downhill, but at Bailey there is Crow Hill. It is two miles of 7% grade with several sharp curves. It is one of the worst down hills in Colorado and many truckers have either ended up in the river at the bottom, over the edge on one of the sharp curves or in the middle of Bailey at the bottom but we were going up and I had to climb it with a bad engine. I knew that if I should by some miracle make the top of Crow Hill in another twenty miles or so there was Schaefer's Crossing.

Schaefer's Crossing is about a four mile uphill climb and 5 to 6% grade. From the top of Schaefer's Crossing it is mostly downhill all the way to Denver, through Turkey Creek Canyon with a lot of sharp curves but by this time I felt comfortable going downhill.

We made Crow Hill and Schaefer's Crossing and met my brother in Conifer, Colorado. We transferred the boys into my brother's car and Jan and I started out for home through Turkey Creek Canyon. We had some pretty exciting moments and I had to use the clutch on several occasions to hold me back but the engine held and by the time we reached the Interstate that goes through Denver I had every confidence that my good old Dodge was going to make it, I even managed to take our borrowed trailer back. The next week I went about finding another engine and installing it.

# **Chapter 9**

Harvest was fast approaching and I had always tried to help Mom and Dad at this time. Going back to the farm in Holyoke would also give us a good opportunity to get our new trailer house ready to move, we still had to move it from the property where dad had bought it. Harvest came and went and during those two weeks we had also managed to pull our new trailer house to dad's farm using one of his tractors.

Like most all summers this one went way to fast. I had given a lot of thought as how to get the camp trailer and the mobile home where we wanted them by not going across the dam and a good amount of thought to the electric and heating systems when we got the mobile home to our property.

We had made a few more trips to paradise and had gotten our camp trailer to the west side of the pond. The access road had been built to our property from the main road and made it a lot easier to access but on two occasions we encountered mountain showers and being a new road the mud made it almost impassable.

With any new area it takes awhile before you learn the lay of the land. The main road across the development west to the San Isabel National Forest line was about two and one half miles from our property. The last mile going west was the same as the Old Cow road to highway 285 only now graded with culverts and ditches, I had driven the road two or three times and had seen where the old hay buck road crossed it. I walked the old road from the new road across Cals Creek to the old hay buck. At the top of the hill I could turn right and follow the brink of that hill to our property. It was a very easy and gentle route to follow and would make it possible to get our camp trailer and trailer house to the other side of the creek without using the dam. It was on one of these last trips that I had pulled the camp trailer using this route to the west side of our creek and had hooked it into our sewer making life easier.

Jan had pretty much laid out the site for the trailer on our property. Not knowing how long it would take to build a cabin, I felt I should make footers and tie down rings to set the mobile home on and secure it. On some of our previous trips to paradise I had poured the concrete footers complete with tie downs by this time I was getting pretty good at mixing concrete in a wheelbarrow. When dad gave me an old cement mixer he had it was like a second Christmas.

We decided to use one of dad's farm trucks to pull the trailer house to our property. He built a frame assembly on the back of his 1967 International truck and installed the hitch to pull it. The truck had a sixteen-foot bed and I did not miss this opportunity to use all of it.

We wanted the trailer house raised about three feet off the ground level so we loaded concrete blocks, railroad ties and anything else we could find that we thought we might use for setting the trailer, the cement mixer went on the truck too.

We had decided to make our trip the end of August. That worked well for dad it was after wheat harvest and before fall planting and corn harvest. I took my week's vacation and Jan arranged time off from her job. We had managed to put away some savings to help pay for the trip.

We left the farm with our caravan; it's approximately three hundred and sixty miles from Mom and Dad's farm to Cactus Acres. Our trip to paradise was full of back roads and shortcuts. Because of the length of the truck and trailer from I-76 at Brush Colorado we went south on State Highway 71 to Limon, Colorado and I -70 where we could get onto Highway 24 to Colorado Springs, then on to Hartsel and Cactus Acres. Trouble was that at Limon, Colorado there is this big Colorado State check station we had to stop "no way around" and of course they were not too thrilled about our caravan and especially our somewhat over length truck and trailer combination.

After some long explaining they let us go but only after buying an over lengths permit. Thank God they didn't weigh us or I probably would've had some more unloading and storing to do and my first two attempts hadn't been too successful.

At that time Highway 24 went through Colorado Springs with no bypasses. About half way through the city we found ourselves with a police escort. The truck was twenty-two feet long, the trailer sixty feet long and the hitch about another three feet. The legal limit at that time was sixty feet and we were almost ninety feet but we had our over length permit, sometimes things do work out. We had quite a traffic jam going on behind us so they just helped us get out of town.

With the load I had put on Dad's truck, I am sure we were overweight which didn't help the long uphill pull on highway 24 from Manitou Springs to Divide. We were in first gear going about two or three mph. At that time highway 24 from Manitou through the canyon was a two-lane road with no pullouts for about nine miles it follows Fountain Creek and is very narrow and winding. By the time we were two miles into the canyon we could not see the end of the traffic behind us, I have no idea how far traffic was backed up probably clear to Colorado Springs by the time we got to our first pull out. The first few vehicles honked and gave us some kind of hand signals but the majority that past us probably did not  have a clue what the holdup had been so went right on by.

We ate our lunch and by that time it was 2.00 P.M. and there was still a steady stream of vehicles going passed us. We more than likely would have gotten a citation for closing a U.S. Highway, but the highway patrol probably did not know what had caused it and could not have gotten up to us anyway.

I was following dad and the trailer house and pulling a loaded trailer, Mom, Jan and the kids were in the van bringing up the rear. We needed to get back on the road so I made a plan, as soon as there was a break in traffic Mom would pull the van onto the highway and stop long enough for Dad and me to get back on the road. Maybe that has some bearing as to why people will not let you into traffic today and I'll bet you thought they were just being rude!

Once on the road again we figured with no complications we could make the Promised Land before dark, or at least Hartsel and the serenity of the county road and away from traffic. Once out of Fountain Canyon the road was wide enough for us to pull far right and there were not as many curves thus allowing traffic to get past us on a regular basis.

From the top of Wilkerson Pass you get a panoramic view of upper South Park, the Collegiate Peak Range, and the Mosquito Range with

Buffalo Peaks in the foreground. It is only about fourteen miles to Hartsel and is a straight flat drive from the bottom of Wilkerson Pass. The west side of Wilkerson Pass is only two miles down but a steep grade with four or five curves. Dad put the old International in granny low which by now had gotten a pretty good workout and headed down. Most all truckers will tell you down hill is the most dangerous driving with the weight of the trailer house pushing him and the weight of the load we knew it would be a long and dangerous trip down.

I went ahead to find an area to pull out going down where dad could get stopped and cool the brakes and rest the engine. There were two good spots, probably made just for that reason. We got to the bottom with no problem and on to the county road. At present we know the name of this road as Park County Road 53, back then it was known as Wagon Tongue Road a lot of old timers still call it that to this day. The county had graded it to within about eight miles of Badger Creek development although very rocky it was a vast improvement over the old Cow Road.

It was dark by the time we got to Cactus Acres, but rather than wait till morning to take the trailer through Cals Creek and on to our property we made the decision to bring the trailer in the back way yet that evening, our reasoning being we felt there would be less traffic to contend with, truth was I doubt there had been a vehicle on the road for a week or longer. We sent mom and the kids on over to the camp trailer at the -"Y"- and we kept going up the hill on the main road. The -"Y"- is where the road to Cactus Acres cuts off from the main road. I led the way with the pickup and dad followed but with the long trailer we had a difficult time turning off of the main road on to the old trail we did it, but it took a lot of jockeying back and forth.

I made it with the pickup through Cals Creek and stopped about one hundred yards ahead by the old hay buck just in time to see dad with the trailer house stopped in the middle of the creek. The banks on either side of the creek were high enough to high center the long trailer house. The front of the trailer hooked to the truck was setting flat on the ground on one side of the creek with the back of the trailer setting on the other side the trailer wheels were about a foot off the creek bottom. After analyzing our situation dad got in the pickup and rode over to the camp trailer with me. After informing Mom and Jan of our situation,

Jan and the boys decided they wanted to spend the night in our new home, after all it was close to the water and pretty level at that.

At breakfast the next morning Dad had pretty much laid out the plan on how we were to get it across the creek. We had unloaded the trailer and pickup after breakfast and with the whole crew went back to rescue our home. It was a neat place to have the trailer unless there was a flood but unfortunately it was not our land.

The truck was pretty much stuck as when Dad had high centered the trailer he had tried to pull it on through. By the time he had decided that he was stuck, the tires were about a foot and one half deep and the hitch was buried in two feet of mud. With the jacks and railroad ties from the truck and logs from the old holding pen we went to work. By 2:00 P.M. we had the truck and trailer house jacked up high enough to build a plank road under the trailer house and the rear tires of the truck. We lowered the whole mess to our plank road and with a few prayers and everyone with crossed fingers to our surprise it pulled right out and on to the Promised Land.

We spent the rest of that day cleaning up the mess on Cals Creek rescuing our much needed railroad planks, washing the mud off the jacks and pry bars and cutting up the logs from the log plank road for fire wood for the weekend. It's a funny thing about working in mud, after you roll around in it for a while and mix it with a little grass you just kind of ignore it, or as Dad would say, "mud grass and ass". Thank God for the pond but even in August it was a pretty cold bath.

After supper we were all wore out, Jan the kids and I slept in the trailer house and Mom and Dad in the camp trailer. It was the second night in our new house and the next morning the kids admitted missing the sound of the running creek under the trailer.

The next day was spent setting the trailer house and by evening we had it jacked up and in place on the footers. The big truck was unloaded again and the wheels and axles were removed from the trailer, Dad was going to build a machine trailer from the axles. Although it seemed like a good idea at the time, it proved to be a real problem in later years when we tried to sell it, we had no way to move it. That evening with our new generator running, we hooked up a floodlight we had brought up and had a campfire with a yard light, we were down town!

The nights at this altitude and being far away from any other lights and in the middle of nowhere, you can look up into the amazing star lit heavens. If you have never had the opportunity you can't imagine it, if you have you know what I mean. To this day when friends and relatives stay over they will spend hours just looking at the galaxies above and even with an inexpensive telescope you can see the mountain ranges on the moon and the shadows they produce we have had over the years friends visit to see the space shuttle and now the space station. The down side is when you are laying there in the dark looking up, the coyotes get to yapping and it seems like they are setting next to you, it will make the short hair on your neck stand straight up, that pretty much ends the stargazing. As a child we had a lot of coyotes come into the farmyard so it never really bothered me, but Jan and the kids had a whole different outlook on it.

Mom and Dad needed to get back so they left rather early the next morning. That day I finished with the tie downs and got steps and a porch made for the front door. The rest of the week was spent skirting in the bottom of the trailer with the lumber and nails from my scavenging operations, the task was made easier since I had the new generator to power my saws and drills.

# **Chapter 10**

Until 1998 there was no communication of any kind anywhere within twenty miles of our area, at that time there were no cell phones and even today there is no cell service. By the 80's satellite phones were available but they were totally out of our financial capabilities. In the early 80's one of the residents who had built in 1975 had acquired a short wave radio that could get into the Park County Sheriff's department. With no way of our own to communicate, we had no way of knowing if Mom and Dad had made it home and were okay. It gives you a very insecure feeling knowing if you needed help there was none unless you could drive to the nearest town.

A very good example of pioneer type communications happened in 1987 when a good friend and neighbor that lived approximately two miles from us suddenly died while eating his supper meal. They had a friend visiting who, after several attempts of trying to resuscitate him to no avail, laid him on the floor. After going to the neighbor that had the radio and finding him gone they came to our place. Jan and I went over but by that time there wasn't much to do but console his wife. I left to go to Buena Vista for a phone but as I went past Grumpy's place his light was on, he had just gotten home. He radioed the Park County Sheriff's office, it was about 8:00 P.M. and I went back over to wait. The first Sheriff arrived around 10:30 P.M., came in and saw the situation and called for an ambulance. They arrived with another Sheriff around 1:00 A.M., after another hour or so they called for the coroner. It turns out that at that time Park County didn't have a coroner and was using Jefferson County's. They had to come from Golden Colorado a distance of some one hundred and twenty miles. They arrived around 7:00 A.M., did what needed to be done and finally left with the body all the while his wife a few friends and myself had a few departing toddies that gave the departed a good head start on the here after.

That should be the end of the ordeal but it was only the starting. I'm not going into detail on the next five days but a sample of what his wife and a few of all of us went through, was that same day we went to make arrangements for the remains and no one seemed to be able to find him. It went down hill from there but in the end and after the cremation he was given a fine send off and is well remembered to this day.

I had made a pigtail cord to plug the generator into the electrical system of the trailer thus giving us lights while the generator was running. Because the trailer had been in a rural area it was already set up for propane, thus making the furnace, hot water heater, stove and oven ready for use. A hot water heater is really of no use without water pressure and unless you run the generator twenty four hours a day or have a good solar system in cold weather a forced air furnace it of little use as well, so all I really had was a cook stove and oven.

There are two terms I have used that needs to be clarified for those not familiar with rural living. A pigtail is just an electric cord with a fitting on each end to connect two electrical devices. Propane is a by-product of crude oil refining but must be in a pressurized container for transport or usage. It is used widely in rural areas for heat and cooking but unlike fuel oil it is under pressure, therefore requiring specialized tanks and equipment for storage and use.

The first order of business was to eliminate the furnace and hot water heater; with these gone it gave us more room and an extra closet for storage.

Camp trailers uses three types of power, Propane for heat and lights, 12volt batteries for lights and water pumps and heater blowers and a 110volt system made to pig tail into a grid where available. There was not much about solar then although if you really wanted to you could find a few companies that could help. Mostly it was for a hot water heating systems, for on grid supplement, very expensive and not too reliable it really was not usable if you were totally off grid as is our case.

I went to a used camper outlet and bought two propane lights basically all they are is the top of a propane camp lantern only made to attach to a wall. I ran a gas line from the main line of the trailer to each of the lights and put them in a location so the light could be used throughout the trailer house at night. A by-product of the lights is the heat, approximately 1200 BTU's each; you must install them so as not to pose a fire hazard to wall or ceiling. By the time we left from our vacation we had night lights and lights to cook and read by.

We had also driven around the new project or what we could of it, as there were only three roads built. We saw where others had bought land and were settling. There were two or three camp trailers around and several campfire rings and other signs of civilization but we had encountered no one.

By the time we had to leave I had the porch built, the bottom of the trailer closed in and lights installed. I had even built in under the trailer an area to install batteries at a future date and a place to put the generator while we were gone. Jan had not been able to wash clothes and the only baths that were taken was accomplished by heating water on the stove and standing in an old washtub that we brought up just for that purpose. Our food supply was down to making bread a real challenge at that altitude but we had pancakes, veggies, and potatoes and seemed to be no worse for the wear. It amazed us that we had not yet had our property for a year and we started loading up to go back to Denver we almost filled the trailer with trash, dirty clothes and I really just don't know what all.

Old habits are hard to break like locking doors, hiding tools and belongings and although I had built an area under the trailer I loaded the generator to take back to Denver for fear that someone would steal it. I loaded all of my tools even the nails, although we had only seen two vehicles in all the time we were there, one I am sure was lost and the other was a salesman with his new clients he was impressed by our progress and though we appreciated his compliments it was obvious they were meant to impress his prospective buyers, I don't think it worked as we never saw them again.

After my lumber problems I really thought that when we returned we probably would not have any furniture left in the trailer. The fact is however that any one up there was either a salesman, Mr., Hutcheson's employees putting in roads, ranchers or some poor sole so lost they probably couldn't have found up and would have had no interest in our treasures only wanting to find their way back to civilization.

After our first taste of remote living it was obvious that I didn't have a clue as to what was really needed to be done before we could actually move up there and live in a somewhat comfortable fashion. It was October before we could get back to our paradise and my good old '59' Dodge had made it to Mom and Dad's and was getting me to work and back. By that time we had accumulated a lot more priceless scavenged material and of course all my tools, the generator, marine batteries and I had bought two one hundred pound propane bottles.

It seemed 4:00 A.M. in the morning had become our starting time and of course this time was no exception. We were taking highway 285 and just about to top out on Turkey Creek Canyon when all hell broke loose. This time I knew a rod had gone through the engine block, it made so much smoke that it looked like half the mountain was on fire. I got Jan and the kids away from it because I did not know if the whole thing was going to blow up or just burn down.

It turned out it was just hot oil hitting cold pavement, Thank God! I stood to lose all of my tools, priceless generator, and junk along with two one hundred pound fully loaded propane bottles that if exploded would have taken out half the county, again I had averted a disaster.

I called my brother to rescue us and although he had never been to our property by now he was getting to know about every boulder in Turkey Creek Canyon just from the many times rescuing me. The brakes on the old truck still worked so I had him tow me all the way home. I figured it was time for retirement for my old truck so that winter we pulled it to Mom and Dad's farm cut it in half and made a trailer out of it.

I used every reasonable argument in the book to get Jan to agree to another vehicle. The biggest reason was that with both of us working we needed two vehicles. Of course there were always public transportation, friends, and bicycles but somehow these alternatives were conveniently lost in my reasoning. I found a 1968 Jeep Commando, they only made this model for three or four years and it didn't take long to find out why, it seems my choices weren't the best but I now owned it so had to make the best of it but I had a 4-wheel drive and I had my own trailer now.

# **Chapter 11**

We watched the weather and in the middle of November made our last visit of the year to paradise. We just took the jeep and the food we needed for an overnight trip. All went well, but we liked to froze to death in our trailer with no heat and no generator. We did have the two propane lights and though they gave off heat we didn't notice except there was no frost on the walls close to them. We skated on our pond, even though I didn't know how thick the ice was but the discharge end of the creek through the culvert pipe was just a column of ice. The kids had a lot of fun as did Jan and I. We had a huge bonfire going most of the day and well into the evening as it was the only heat we had.

That winter I spent designing a storage battery electric system although I had purchased two marine batteries I had not gotten them to paradise. I chose marine batteries because they were not only made to start a motor but for storage to use for lights, pumps, etc. on a boat.

Today most systems uses 6volt storage batteries designed for solar systems, but this was way before that type of technology was commonplace. There were only two companies in the Denver area that even handled off grid applications and after visiting with them it was obvious they were made for the very wealthy individuals or large companies that could afford them. I did gain a lot of knowledge from visiting with them and by studying the literature they supplied.

The first thing I learned was the difference between a converter and an inverter. Confused? You should have been in my shoes, I couldn't even spell converter or inverter let alone understand their application, you can learn a lot if you do a lot of listening instead of a lot of talking. It's really very simple, a converter takes 110volt AC, or common household current and converts it to DC power. A good example would be your cell phone charger. An inverter does just the opposite it changes DC currant to AC current or using the current from you 12volt DC car batteries changes it to 110volt AC household current.

I learned that the more batteries you had the more storage and the longer you could go, depending on usage, before you needed to recharge them. Another advantage of a marine battery over a regular battery was recharging them. A car battery doesn't last very long if you continually discharge and recharge it, while a marine battery won't be affected nearly as badly.

There are two ways of connecting batteries together. You can maintain the same voltage by hooking the batteries in parallel and by adding batteries you increase storage capacity. You can increase the output voltage by putting them in a series configuration, but the storage capacity stays the same. With two 12volt batteries hooked in series you can get a 24volt system and with four 12volt batteries hooked in series you can get a 48volt system.

If you don't hook them together correctly they can blow up, so if you're not familiar with how to hook them up properly have it done professionally. I won't belabor this point but I hooked my batteries in parallel to maintain a 12volt output. This allows me to use automotive and marine type 12volt lights, fans, pumps, etc. in my trailer house.

At that time I could not afford an inverter so I decided to use only 12volt and have two or three outlets that would be used direct from the generator. That would give us outlets for a vacuum cleaner, electric heater, or other small kitchen appliances. All I had to do now was to get it to the Promised Land and see if it would actually work. I understand this is confusing but this same system can easily be applied in part to almost any home and as you will learn can be of great value in case of a power outage.

The next summer was spent getting the bills paid and installing all my winter projects in our trailer. I made a box and insulated it for the batteries as I had read that you should keep them at temperatures ranging from 50°F to 70°F for the best performance. I installed the batteries under the trailer close enough to the electrical connection so that I could run the electric cord (pigtail) from batteries to the trailer supply thus giving the 12volt DC power throughout. Somehow I needed to keep the batteries charged and at the time the only affordable means was a battery charger which takes 110volt electricity to operate, thus the generator.

I changed the light bulbs from regular 110volt AC to 12v DC bulbs readily available at a camper outlet and wah-la! I had lights in every room of our trailer. The problem with using hard wiring for 12 volt is line loss making the lights dimmer than normal.

After you live off grid for a while you get real good at only using lights and/or appliances only when needed. When the batteries needed to be charged we would run the generator and while it was running we would fill our water tank do the washing any other chores that required 110 volt 60cycle AC.

Our water system is extremely unique. Although we had drilled a well it was really just a waste of time. To the northwest of our trailer there was an underground spring that runs from the bottom of the hill down past the trailer to the southeast to badger Creek. We weren't aware of it until Mr. Hutcheson cut the stream banks for the pond. When the pond filled as with all water, it found a new static level rising to the underground level of the spring. After a year or so it became very apparent by looking at the Saw grass just where the spring started and ran across our property. It turned out that we had positioned the house perfectly as the spring crossed about eighty feet in front of it.

My eldest brother had gone to college and by that time had a very good job overseas in Germany. When I told him of the spring and its location he sent me plans to install a French drain system. It seems they are common in that part of the world used to drain wetland caused by springs. Basically it is a specially designed trench cut through the middle of the underground spring above the area to be drained. The trench has to be dug to the depth where the spring flows from the ground freely. I had to dig mine about fourteen feet deep because of the way my land laid. You put about two feet of rock in the bottom; we had plenty of rock readily available. You then place something like slotted PVC pipe like you use in a sewer leach line, on top of the stone. You then add another layer of rock add another run of PVC slotted pipe add more fine stone and fill the trench to ground level with soil. You then connect the top pipe or collector with the bottom pipe or collector and run a solid pipe from the connection at a slight downhill grade to the drainage ditch but since I was using this system to capture our potable water supply I need to connect to an underground holding tank.

Because of my ground level my holding tank needed to be buried only about nine feet deep to get the correct level. I put my intake pipe about eight inches above the tank bottom so any sediment would accumulate on the tank bottom and not enter my discharge pipe. After finding the static level in the tank which was accomplished by letting the tank fill until the underground spring found its level in the tank I installed a discharge pipe in the tank slightly below that level. By doing this when the tank was full the water would run through it thus keeping fresh running water in the tank and no sediment or germs, it acts like a line purification system. I then ran a four inch line about a foot off the bottom of the tank at an angle to under the house.

I installed a 12 volt demand pump like that used in most camper applications and ran a three-quarter-inch line with a check valve on the pickup end down the four inch line and into the tank. Now every time you open a water line anywhere in the house it automatically pumps the water and when the faucet is closed it pumps to pressure and stops just like in a camper or R.V. The best part is I never have to pump water into a tank and I always have about three hundred gallons of usable water, the recharge is about forty gallons an hour so I've never run it dry to this day.

By insulating the tank with four inch foam insulation and for the intake pipe I made a box around the four inch pipe using the same insulation. The water running through the tank won't freeze but the inlet and sides of the tank could that's why the insulation. The inlet froze up the first year so I wrapped the three quarter inch pickup line with heat tape and pipe insulation. The next year it got down to -52 degrees for about three days and it froze but all I had to do was start the generator and plug-in the heat tape. I had it thawed out in about an hour. I used a freeze/thaw line from the pump to the tank so it would not break when or if it freezes. The best part of the system is you never have to pump water that requires electricity and uses only 12volt DC direct current from my batteries using little electric power.

That's probably more about a French drain system than anyone should even have to know and it only applies if you have an on site spring but I'm pretty proud of that accomplishment so had to share it with you.

As you can imagine by now we pretty much had our paradise going the way we had envisioned it.

# **Chapter 12**

With the propane for lights and cooking, 12volt power for lights, lots of very good water for bathing, toilet, dishes, and the washing machine. All I needed now was a heating system and a good clothesline. Well okay, maybe a few other things too.

I should inject here that the first three years we hauled our drinking water up from Denver it took us that long to realize that Mr. Barber the developer had drilled the community well complete with hand pump giving us probably the best water one could find anywhere.

By 1973 and 1974 we would go the twenty two miles into Buena Vista for our needs. The Forest Road had only been graded maybe once or twice and was somewhat better but the bog was still a challenge when wet. Although graded it only made all the traffic go in a one-lane trail in an extremely muddy area so when people got stuck they would leave some very deep and long ruts to manage around so the only time we would go that way was dry weather or when frozen.

The Forest Road not only offers some of the most beautiful scenery one can imagine, but if traveled in early-morning or evening there is an abundance of wildlife. It's not unusual to see deer, elk, mountain sheep, turkeys, antelope, bears and mountain lions. I don't know of anyone that has lived here for two years or more that hasn't experienced all of these.

The first few years we owned Paradise in the winter we would get quite a few elk on our land. Having two streams and Badger Creek being a warm spring that never freezes, it gave deer and elk a good source of water during the winter. I'll share one memory with you that will really bring home the point. In the winter of 72 – 73 (I can't remember the exact date) we were up for the weekend. It was snowing lightly when we went to bed and being an early riser, around 5:00 A.M I was laying in bed not wanting to get up yet as it was cold and I could see my breath when not under the comforters, I kept hearing these grunts and scratching noises. I awakened Jan and shushed her thinking maybe she could figure out the noise. Of course she was frightened to death thinking bears, lions or whatever. We lay there for quite some time listening. Sometimes it was loud and then seemed to fade, but the scratching though not consistent seemed close.

By predawn that's when it's almost light and almost dark I'd had all I could take. I got out of bed put on my slippers and opened the curtain on the one window in the bedroom only to see the biggest elk butt in the world. Jan and I went from window to window on the south side of the trailer only to be greeted by the same site only different elk. By light we could make out about two hundred or so elk all within one hundred to two hundred and fifty feet of our trailer. They surrounded the truck were on the dam, just everywhere. These are the sort of thing you just don't see often and are the memories that keep you coming up and wanting more.

In the spring of 1974 Jan's son was starting the fourth grade in school our oldest would be starting kindergarten. Even back then there was a lot of school violence, Jan's son almost daily would have to run home just to keep from being picked on or worse and on one occasion beat up. I know I had never had that experience and remember thinking it was no wonder kids couldn't learn or like school it was more like sending your child off to a prison camp.

Although I'd had several promotions and was in management at the truck line and Jan was doing payroll for a pretty large company we both knew a lot better life existed in a small farm town. We sold our home and with help of dad's trucks moved east.

We knew that we wouldn't be able to get to Cactus Acres much because summer is when you really work on a farm but the kids came first and in no way could we get our kids to school and back at Cactus Acres so our only other option was Holyoke, Colorado.

I had several jobs working with farmers or farm companies and dad didn't need my help except at harvest time and sure couldn't afford to hire me.

In 1975 we got a letter from one of the families living in Badger Creek Ranch telling us that a flood had gone through and taken out our dam and pretty much everything else. It must've been a doozy, because where Badger Creek ends it dumps into the Arkansas River just above Howard, Colorado and it also took out half of Howard.

That was in late July but we couldn't get back up there until late August, July and August is harvest time in eastern Colorado. When we did go we were greeted with no dam only a little jetty protruding from either side of the creek. The concrete spillway too was all but gone as was the shell-casing culvert. We had planted some trees and bushes along the inlet side and dam bottom, they too were gone probably in Kansas via the Arkansas River.

Our plan to raise the trailer three foot above ground proved to be a good move nothing had bothered it. What we did notice was that the stream had doubled or tripled its normal running size. After walking upstream we could see why, when the wall of water got to our dam it must've stopped it long enough to create an undertow as one hundred yards or so upstream from the dam on a curve, it had washed out a hole about ten feet long and four to five feet deep to bedrock opening up the flow of the stream.

We hadn't locked the trailer when we left but had put most of our tools, wheelbarrow, wagon, and cement mixer under or in it, to our surprise everything was just as we had left it, the batteries without maintenance had frozen and rendered them useless but even the generator was still there. We only had three days to make that trip and most of that was spent driving. It takes about eight hours to drive from Holyoke to Cactus Acres. After only one night we said goodbye and headed home.

# **Chapter 13 **

By late 1977 we had ventured into our own business, as any business owner will tell you it's a seven day week and twenty hours a day job. So we didn't get back to Paradise until 1979 when we were told it needed to be painted and repaired.

We did have one life experience in 1977 I should share with you. It had a profound impact on how we built and the appliances we furnished our cabin with along with what one really needs to not just survive but live comfortably in the off grid situation at Cactus Acres in later years. In March of 1977 a spring storm came through our area in Holyoke Colorado. That in and of it self was not unusual but what was unusual was how it occurred. It started out as an ice storm in the late evening by midnight it had accumulated ice on everything about four to six inches deep. That's not unusual in the New England states but I don't think it had ever happened before or since in the northeastern corner of Colorado. We could hear the loud popping cracking sound of the power lines and trees breaking from the weight of the ice, it was almost constant.

We had purchased about three acres of land that from the teens to the fifty's had been an old gas station. It was eight miles north of town on Highway 385 between Julesburg, Colorado and Holyoke, Colorado on a correction line. If you were traveling south to north and if you missed the curve you would have hit our house.

We had huge trees to the west and north and east of the House in three to five rows the length of the property. I had just added on to the House so it was quite large about thirty one hundred square foot. I had also raised the new roof on it so it was over sixteen feet high at the peak. After the ice storm came the snow and wind, a real blizzard. When I remodeled I was talked into, as was the trend going all electric. The electric company gave incentives at that time the more you used the cheaper it was. We had put in a rather large fireplace on one wall of the living room. The living room was about twenty five foot by thirty foot but the ceilings were low because I had planned to make a second story above it. If all this seems insignificant it's not, it's probably what saved a lot of lives.

About 3:00 A.M. we were awakened by someone hollering for us. I got to the kitchen door and a friend who was a snow plow operator for the state was standing there. Neil was a big man, 6'4" to 6'6" and very muscular covered with snow, wet and very cold.

He informed us that he had made it to our curve he had been traveling north to south toward Holyoke and had been stuck and dug himself out several times since around midnight. He had picked up three oil drillers who had been stranded along the road and had them in his truck cab, he had also found a Christian musical group that had gotten stranded they had a truck and three cars. The truck and one of the cars had gotten stuck in a snowdrift and had been abandoned. In the remaining two cars they had tried to follow behind his snow plow but had gotten those stuck in the snow as well as the snow plow, there were twenty-one people in them.

I hope you never see a plain's blizzard one cannot begin to explain the constant roar and utter complete helplessness you incur. If caught in the open your chances of survival is slim and if you leave your vehicle it's almost zero. For Neil to be standing in our kitchen was a real testimonial to his strength and courage as a matter of fact I really thought that it wasn't all that bad or he wouldn't have tried it at all.

We made arrangements to go out and get those who were stranded back to our home. With an all electric home, the power lines falling like matchsticks it made for a very dark and cold house. We had a few flashlights and he had one, we headed out on our rescue mission. I had gotten only about ten feet from the door and found myself up to my waist in wind packed snow. That is when the severity of the situation hit me. In a blizzard you have to holler to be heard even at two or three feet apart, Neil told me that just fifteen minutes before it was only knee deep there that news really made us speed up our efforts, as in an hour or so it could bury the cars.

I thought I knew that area like the back of my hand but the blowing and drifting snow around the buildings and the depths of the drifts in the dark gave a whole different perspective to where I was. My sense of direction has always been very keen and it didn't let me down this time. Neil while in the house wasn't really sure where on the curve he was. The curve is a long lazy one probably about four hundred yards long. It went straight along our property then curved again to an eight-mile straight road into town. Neil knew the road better than I or anyone else as he plowed and maintained it for years. The trees and buildings of our place were on the west side of the road and the blizzard was what we call a wrap-around coming out of the southwest. He figured with the wind direction that it had drifted the road closed probably one hundred yards or so to the north of our tree line.

From the kitchen door I went to the southeast where the building that housed our business was located. I followed it to where it ended I knew that there was an opening of about fifty feet to the tree line on the extreme east side of our property. The ditch was cut out about six feet deep and about sixty feet to the highway with a gentle slope on both sides we left the building and went what I thought was straight east to the tree line but after about five minutes I realized I had been going up as well as East. Neil was behind me and I could see the dim outline of his light which was slightly lower than me, it should have been even or higher depending upon if I was in the ditch. I turned to meet Neil and asked where the trees were he hadn't seen them either and agreed that we should have. We decided to go north that maybe we had gone southeast instead of straight east.

After only three or so minutes we felt we were going down. Sure enough the lights proved us right still no trees and Neil motioned to keep to the northeast and follow the drift down which was a good move, about five minutes later I actually ran into the windshield of the highway truck. The wind and snow had pretty much been to our backs getting there but on the trip back the wind would be directly in our faces.

The oil drillers were glad to see us but not real worried as they were pretty much local and had been through a few Wyoming blizzard's, the musical group however was totally in a panic, not that I blamed them because in their cars there were twenty one people in two small four door sedans, that's pretty cozy and I don't think they'd had a bathroom break for many hours. The group was the Regeneration from Nashville, Tennessee. Only two or three were from rural areas and most were from pretty affluent families in the South. All were seventeen to twenty five years of age and were dressed in dress pants and ties or skirts and high heels they were very well groomed and looked very professional. They had managed to get their coats, hats or scarves before abandoning their truck and other car so they had a little protection.

Neil put me in the lead while he took up the rear with a three drillers spaced in between the singers. One of the singers was from a farm in Steen, Minnesota he too was placed in a chaperone position. By this time it was getting light; by this I mean it was a dull gray but we could make out shapes and people at a distance of five to ten feet so we didn't need our flashlights.

The progress was slow as the drifts were now higher and the snow was in our faces the snow felt like sand hitting you. I led them back following pretty much the same path that Neil and I had used to find them. From the front of the plow truck I went southwest I found my tree line or should I say the treetops, Neil and I had walked over the trees and they were about twenty to twenty five feet high.

At that point I knew exactly where we were and about halfway down the drift I ran into the top of our workshop. It was about that time that one of the girls the second one back, just laid down. She had been doing a lot of praying all the way and no doubt with a short dress and high heels she was close to freezing. She had succumbed to the notion that she was going to just die there I picked her up as I knew we were only about sixty feet from the east door into our living room. The snow had blown clean between the shop and the house so that the area was wide open as far as the snow went and being on the east side of the house there was very little wind when I got within fifteen foot of it, we got everyone in the house although not warm it felt like heaven.

Jan had the fireplace going we had put in a pretty good supply of wood before the storm. She had done a complete appraisal of our situation knowing she was about to be swarmed with twenty-five guests and our own family of five.

The problem with depending on electricity is when you don't have it. An electric pump for the well so no water and electric stove so no cooking and electric blower for the furnaces so no heat and no lights. We had the refrigerator full of food as was the chest freezer because Jan and mom canned from the gardens each year we had veggies, potatoes, chicken, turkey and broth Jan was so organized it just made me proud to say I was her husband.

One of the worst problems was the bathrooms or toilets, with no water you can't flush and with thirty people it doesn't take long well you get the picture. There is also the drinking water problem, not having a stove we had no way to boil water for drinking and had no water to boil anyway, we were in a fix.

Being on the main highway we were the first to have gotten our underground phone cable in the year before so as miracles do happen we had a phone. By around 10:00 A.M. Neil had been able to contact his regional office in Sterling, Colorado. They had gotten a little snow and had gotten a few reports of the conditions from Haxtun, Colorado east and had a hard time believing we had drifts that deep and was still snowing and blowing. He had also gotten hold of the emergency services in Holyoke and informed them of our situation but they could do little as there was still a good blizzard going on.

By 8:00 A.M. I knew something had to be done about getting water. I knew by looking out the windows that the house was pretty nearly buried all you could see was snow but on the north side of the house is the back door complete with window and the kid's bedroom windows. I could tell the wind vortex had removed the snow and there was a space about four feet or so along the west side to the corner and the north side where it was bare ground from there the snow went up over the eves of the house.

I opened the kitchen door only to see snow packed against the storm door. It open outward so I broke out the bottom glass and then began getting snow and melting it on the fireplace in pans that Jan was setting in and around the fire and at the same time making a refrigerator so all our food wouldn't spoil.

Most of the Regeneration had found sofas, beds or the floor and gone to sleep. Jan had many blankets so they could warm up and stay warm I remember one fellow slept all day we checked on him occasionally to see if he was dead or not. I took a floor lamp and stripped both ends of it and bent it so I could wedge it over the fire between the sides of the firebox and used two metal coat hangers fashioned into hooks, that made it so Jan could hang a big pot on it to make our food, one meal a day but you don't need much when you don't do much.

Jan dumped jars of her canned veggies, potatoes, chicken and turkey broth into a rather large pot, put in her spices and by 3:00 P.M. of that day we had us a king's feast the Regeneration even put that in a song they later wrote and recorded about the blizzard of 77.

By approximately 3:00 P.M. the storm had actually gotten worse the house was pretty much covered and the light was just a dull gray. Neil had been told not to expect the storm to let up until the next day. The National Guard had been called out and was trying to make it to Haxtun, Dailey, Holyoke, and Amherst, Colorado along with the Venango and Grant and Imperial Nebraska areas but was unable to get to any of them and of course no airplanes or helicopters could fly, they asked us to do our best what choice did we have?

The only way you knew it had become night was that the house went from gray to black. With so many people it made it easy to take shifts keeping the fire going and melting snow for our water needs. It takes a lot of snow to make a gallon of water and it takes approximately four to five gallons just for one toilet flush but we had plenty of snow to melt, by then our door cooler was cut out enough that I had taken the storm door completely out of the opening so we were opening the kitchen door and walking into our cooler. We had made snow shelves along each side of the cooler and just took our pans in and scooped them full to melt by the fire.

Although we had made shifts of four people at a time during the night to stoke the fire and melt snow most of the time there were more. We had a lot of games and cards which helped to pass the time; at night they just got a little closer to the fire to make it easier to see the game boards or cards. By early the next morning the last of the wood was put on the fire I was awakened and appraised of the situation. Most of our furniture was hand-me-downs and was getting pretty old so we started with the kid's dressers they were pretty much empty anyway. Everyone there was opposed to the idea but fire was life. With the melted snow water we had been able to flush the toilet several times which was a blessing to all and by using the coffee pot to boil water (we still had the old peculator kind) was able to make some hot chocolate and juice to drink.

By light the next morning it was apparent we didn't have nearly enough furniture to make it through another day. The wood shed was about twenty feet north of the back door which was cleared out enough by the vortex to open the door. The wind wasn't loud now because a lot of the house was covered in snow, but we could tell it was still blowing.

I found a clothesline rope that Jan used in the laundry room to hang clothes on bad days. I tied it to me and with the five other guys looped onto it I started up the snow bank to the eve of the house about sixteen feet or so. When I got to the eve I took my pan shovel and started scooping. Most of it fell back down on top of the guys but they just started pushing it down into the opening along the edge of the house. I had only scooped about five minutes before I broke through the top. It was still blowing very hard and hit my face like rocks I crawled north to where I thought the woodshed was and started to dig down, about two feet down I hit the top of a clothesline post, what are the odds of finding a three inch post top and missing a twelve by ten foot building?

I wasn't sure what end of the clothesline I was on but was almost sure it was the one closest to the wood shed. So I went to my right or east about ten feet and then my left or north about five or eight feet and started digging down again about three feet down I hit the top of the shed I actually got a tear of joy in my eye when I found it. The shed was about seven feet high and had a window in the front, I found the southeast corner went west about six feet and started down, I was right on the window and I used my pan to break it out, by that time the guys had been laying head to toe across the snow for some time. We went back and got reinforcements and formed a human chain from the shed to the house, I pitched it up to the first guy he to the next and so on. In thirty or forty minutes we had the laundry room pretty much filled with wood and all went back in we now had enough wood for a week or so. It took some time for everyone involved to warm up.

We had plenty of clothes all the girls had found clothes that kind of fit, most came from the kid's closets and dressers, we were a motley looking crew but our spirits were high. By this time we had two soup pots going all the time, one cooking and one ready-to-eat. I'm not sure but some of the gals told us later that they thought they had actually gained weight.

Neil was in touch with his office and we were told the storm should end that next night.

The Regeneration sang for us quite a few times during that ordeal and they were very good. They had made quite a few records and eight track tapes and we got to hear most all their recorded songs, we still on occasion listen to their records which brings back all the memories.

By the next morning we were all getting real good at this blizzard living, we had plenty of water a lot of canned food left to eat. By 7:00 A.M. the dark gray went to a bright gray and we couldn't hear any wind. On the west side of the living room was our sliding patio door, but I had not built the patio yet. There was still an area where the eddy currents had cleared the snow out along the house so the guys and I started building stairs up from the patio door to the top of the drift, we emerged into bright sunlight. I think it only took about a minute before everyone was on top of the drift hollering, praying and of course throwing snowballs.

Two of the oil drillers decided to start walking home they lived in Ovid, Colorado, a distance of thirty miles or so. Neil by connecting with his dispatcher in Sterling, Colorado was told there were many life-threatening situations in our area and if we were okay to wait it out until roads were opened and other emergencies were dealt with.

We didn't receive any help that first day but the sunshine and light really helped to lift the spirits of everyone. By this time they had found their cars and the snowplow and although all you could see of them were the trunk and top of the back car, part of the top of the second car the windshield and top of the snowplow. They retrieved some of their belongings from the cars, not that we needed them but it made them feel better.

I had gotten into the shop and found shovels, tools, etc. and went about making things better for our stay. Neil and some of the guys were able to get three pieces of roofing tin that had been buried from behind the shop and laid them on the top of the drift. They placed them in a slightly folded shape so the sun could hit them and we kept putting thin layers of snow on them the snow melted rather quickly and the water ran into a buried five gallon bucket placed at the end, we now had a lot of water. That night everyone could sleep as we didn't need to melt water, but someone got up once in a while to stoke the fire and add a log or two.

By noon of the next day the State had opened highway 285 south from Julesburg to the stalled cars on our curve, we were all there to greet them. In one of the plow trucks, there was quite a convoy of equipment, they had two bags of supplies given them by the two oil drillers, candy bars, doughnuts, bread, lunch meat, canned fruit, and canned beans for our stew, I don't remember everything but what a treasure.

The plow driver had told us that in Julesburg there was not much snow four or five inches, and the drifts were only about a foot or two across the road. By the time they got to within ten miles north of our place they started to get into big drifts. The eleven mile curve had a ten foot drift over two hundred yards long which is why it had taken so long to get this far but our drift was by far the biggest they had encountered and they weren't even going to attempt to plow it with their equipment.

We also found out that Highway 6 from Haxtun into Imperial, Nebraska was still inaccessible by road and the plows were still on Highway 6 west of Holyoke, about seven miles from reaching town. The National Guard was ferrying emergency supplies to several towns using helicopters.

Quite a few people were missing including a pregnant woman and some linemen that worked for the electric company. From the air they could see many farms covered with snow but couldn't tell if the people were in trouble or not, they could also see hundreds of dead cattle. It had become a full-blown rescue effort by state and national emergency services.

In our little corner of the blizzard, the state crew had managed to get the two cars and plow truck out and on the good road headed north. They had also plowed out the Regeneration's van and the other car and had them sitting on the road. Five of the Regeneration guys took one of their cars back to collect the other vehicles and it took about an hour for them to get back. After changing to their original clothes they all headed north for Julesburg and beyond.

That afternoon we were alone in our place, just the five of us but we had a feast on our newfound groceries. It was about an hour after Neil and the other oil driller had left with the highway crew back to Julesburg and the Regeneration had departed, that Jan and I both just broke down. It took Jan and me almost an hour to stop crying but we finally collected ourselves and started looking into the immediate future.

By the afternoon of the next day the National Guard had gotten a D8 Caterpillar dozer to our place from Holyoke, it had taken most of the night and up until 2:00 P.M. the next day to open the eight miles of road to us, twenty to thirty foot drifts were the norm. The dozers would climb to the top of the drift and just start plowing down the other side, turn around and come back. It's hard to believe that snow could pack so tight that it could support the massive machine but it did.

As I mentioned the highway was east of our place and to the south was a county road. Because of all our trees and buildings and the high winds estimated to be sixty to over eighty mph had buried us on all sides. By 5:00 P.M that same day they had the highway open and by midnight they had the county road open, our home was an island in the middle of the snow moat.

Three days later we had power, it was the luck of the draw, we actually had power before many of the towns it seems that when they got the feed line into Holyoke fixed and energized we had power. The line from Holyoke to our corner hadn't gone down because it was a north-south line, any of the east-west lines in the storm area had been decimated, some seven thousand poles and countless miles of wire were needed to complete the repair.

I could write an entire book just on the storm and the aftermath, we found out later the storm covered a large area of eastern Colorado, western Kansas and the south west corner of Nebraska. There were ten lives lost, the pregnant lady and her unborn child were found and later airlifted to an area hospital, the two linemen were found along with eight other linemen, they had made it to nearby farms. Imagine a blizzard during the pioneer days of the West and Midwest, after what we had gone through it gives one a whole new perspective on life.

# **Chapter 14**

When we finally got back to cactus acres, we found it pretty much as it had been when we left it, but needed to be painted. The stairs and porch had been torn nearly apart, apparently by cows as was the skirting. We fixed it the best we could by painting and using what material we had for stairs, skirting, etc., thankfully the generator, furniture, and tools, were still there. Inside we found no rats or signs of mice but the cows had pushed out a louver in one of the louvered glass windows on the door and a bird had found its way in. We were angry, not because of the mess it had made but because it had died and it was the first bluebird we could remember seeing on our property.

We made a few trips off and on but had pretty much decided our home was in eastern Colorado and that we really had no use for our Paradise. In early 1980 we started trying to sell the property. We had a few calls but when they got the directions to get there we never heard from them again .We did have one party that was interested and even looked at it but it turned out all they wanted was the trailer house. With no axles or wheels there was no way to move it so we found we couldn't even get rid of that. Our business had done pretty well by this time but with all the traveling and the boy's school activities, we pretty much forgot about Cactus Acres. We did try to get there at least once a year and some friends got up there occasionally as well.

During the 70s and early 80s, Badger Creek Ranch development had really become a developed community. There were many mobile homes on properties, four or five cabins and at least four full-time residents. Two families were sending their children to school; they would drive the twenty three miles to Hartsel where they would meet the school bus and then another eighteen miles to Fairplay.

By 1977 when we did spend time at Paradise we always tried to make improvements. After the flood of 75 we had contracted an earth excavating company in Guffey, Colorado that specialized in cleanup of stream banks, building ponds, dams and that type of work. The owner was also an engineer so we had him come over and give us some professional help he redesigned the pond and told us how to not only hold water but to control it.

I rented a large front-end loader from Colorado Springs and had it delivered twice! He was so lost the first time he went back home, I led him in the second time. I didn't realize what I had rented until I saw it on his sixteen wheeler the tires were taller than I am. Having been around farm equipment most of my life it really didn't intimidate me but I did need instruction on its operation I figured maybe a two day job but rented it for a week. It cost a pretty good chunk of change but not nearly what the construction company wanted.

The next morning after delivery I couldn't wait to get started. My two sons had brought my pickup and twenty foot trailer the day before. I had one hundred gallons of diesel fuel in two fifty gallon barrels I had also brought up the new culvert. It was forty two feet of twenty-six inch diameter culvert. The design called for a down drop type system whereby the inlet side of the culvert is placed approximately fifteen feet from the bottom of the dam and then goes up to the water level desired, it is buried in the creek bottom and should extend at least ten feet on the discharge side. This design keeps the water from creating a vortex or washing out either end of the dam. By selecting a flexible type culvert all I needed to do to fill the dam when complete was to lift up the inlet end thus making it easy to adjust the water level in the pond, it works as well today as when I installed it. Every two years I drain my pond to help control pondweeds and clean it.

The boys had a little trouble on the way up, about half way in on County Road 53 from Hartsel. Because of the somewhat rocky and rough road, and going a little fast, though that was denied, the trailer came unhooked it ended up in a cow pasture but didn't upset. The barrels of fuel landed on their sides although bent and dented they didn't lose a drop the culvert was still somewhat on the trailer. They are pretty good sized boys and after reconnecting the trailer they managed to reload the fuel and culvert and continued on their journey but at a somewhat slower pace I'm sure.

I got the loader started let it warm up, and went to work; I pushed up a big pile of earth from the bank into the stream bottom. My idea was to just keep dumping earth from one bank to the other keeping it high enough to drive on as I knew the creek bottom was soft and that I could get stuck. On the second dump I felt the front tires start to sink when I was about to make my dump so stopped and dumped the load I backed up to see I had sunk only six inches. I figured it would be okay to go over the dump pull the dirt back to the bank to level it out and get dry dirt where I was working. I drove ahead far enough to lower the bucket and pull the dirt back, the front of my loader just disappeared, I looked down to see the tops of my tires about half of my axles and sinking fast. I'm not going into detail here I was not only stuck, the more I tried to get it out the deeper it got by the time I decided I needed help all I had to do to get out of the cab was open the door and step out onto the dirt, I had buried a four-wheel drive articulated steering front loader. All I had to do was say a prayer and finish burying it the problem was they cost over $100,000 to replace.

That week was spent trying to get the tractor out I had several winch trucks, wreckers, and tractors trying to get it out by the end of the week they hadn't even moved it. With no phone service I had made a lot of trips to Buena Vista, Fairplay and Hartsel. I made another trip to Guffey, and told him of my predicament, I hadn't had any luck with any of my previous tries, but I was assured he could get it out. I agreed to his charges (I really was in no position to negotiate), and waited for his arrival the next day.

He had an old Austin Western road grader but had modified it for his business. By the time he got to Cactus Acres it was almost noon, from Guffey to Cactus Acres is about a forty mile ride so he had actually made good time. He backed up to the cable I had acquisition in my travels and hooked on. He had me put my butt in the seat of the front end loader and by the time I had it started and in gear he had pulled me out. That old Austin Western hadn't even pulled down or smoked, I found out later it was a six wheel direct drive with the biggest diesel engine Cummings made, it was truly a tank. He stayed about an hour using his grader and had leveled out all the banks and had a twenty five foot wide fill over my culvert and across the creek to the other side I finished it the next week. I dug out to the east of the stream and made an island in the pond and a crossing fifteen feet wide on the top of the dam. It turned out really nice but by the time I had paid all the expenses and lost two full weeks from our business I probably could have had a lake instead of a one acre pond. But the pond is still there today and has seen some pretty big floods.

I had purchased a used Cadillac car and in September we decided to spend a night at our paradise. When we got to the Black Dumps on Forest Road 187 we were greeted with a one foot snow drift through the gate just like when we had the old '59' Dodge and had to unload it. I got out and walked it and the road looked clear down the hill on the other side. There had been a vehicle through as there were some old tracks, so I made a run at it. All of a sudden the car went up and there was a terrible grinding of metal sound full length of the car, I made it through and went back to see what had caused the noise. I was greeted by a somewhat scarred up rock about twelve inches high and the size of my head in diameter.

It had completely smashed the exhaust pipe of my low clearance car against the transmission case and a crossover frame support. I found a wood chisel in the trunk and no other tools, after jacking up the car I went about cutting the exhaust by using only the wood chisel and tire wrench. Two hours later it was drivable again with one end of the exhaust pipe wired up with fence wire and a car that sounded like an Indy five hundred race car we made it to Cactus Acres for the night and the next morning. I jacked it up again to see if there was any chance of getting it home, I did some cowboying on it and decided if we left the windows down just maybe we wouldn't all get asphyxiated going home, by the time we got started for home the temperature had risen to a balmy fifteen degrees but at least I hadn't wrecked the heater and at times you could almost feel it on the way home.

On that same trip when we did get to paradise a hundred and fifty to two hundred head of cattle greeted us. They were all around our trailer and all over the dam it was obvious from the damage they had done that they had pretty much made it their home. Now we knew firsthand what dad had meant in our reality grilling about open range.

When we got back home I told dad of our findings. Dad and Mom had long since quit the cattle business and offered me all the fencing I needed to fence the ten plus acres. We brought up the fencing from the farm and back to Denver and by the next spring we were ready to install our fence, we loaded the truck and trailer and headed back to Cactus Acres on a mission.

One of my son's and his wife with some persuasion had agreed to help. I had modified the trailer so I could put a roll of wire on top and by pulling the trailer it should unroll. While the idea had merit the application left a little to be desired as about half way down the hill on the first run the wire broke and because of the tension snapped back with enough force that it almost cut my son in half, Jan and the band aids to the rescue. We scrapped my invention and in about five days had a very nice five-wire fence in place and it is still there to this day. While installing the fence we were greeted by one of our neighbors. We had met him before and after introducing ourselves he informed us we couldn't put up a fence on our property as the subdivision had a perimeter fence and no cows could get on subdivision land. I assured him that they could, they had and they had caused quite a bit of damage to our place. After some not too friendly conversation I told him that under state law it was my responsibility to fence out livestock under the open range law and I intended to do just that. Three weeks later when we were up doing some off grid electrical work, the same herd of cattle greeted us. We took pictures of them on the other side of our fence and set out to find the Badger Creek Bilker. He wasn't at his Shack so we left him a note to come see what all these critters were around our fence, we knew they couldn't be cows as he had assured us that cows couldn't get on Badger Creek Ranch property. We never heard from him again until well into the middle 80s.

# **Chapter 15**

In the fall of 86, after returning home from a trip to Las Vegas at a trade convention associated with our business we were greeted by the news that the federal government had closed our bank. Hindsight is fantastic but in retrospect we just didn't know business. We had no problem getting business we knew how to make a profit and to produce our product but we knew very little about how to handle money investments banking and all the things that make or break you.

1984 – 1987 was the last big recession before 2008. A lot of oil companies went bust as did many farmers there were many banks closed as a result. We had only used one bank for all our business it catered to farmers, therefore when it closed we had no money no credit line and no cash flow, everything came to a halt!

It took about two weeks before we could even find anyone to talk to and when we did we were told that nothing would be done until our account was reviewed and that would be at least one to two months. We went to other banks but what they knew was that all the closed banks assets eventually would be sold for about ten cents on the dollar. This rendered our business worthless and there was no way they would grant a loan not even an operating loan. After about two months of total stress seeing all you had worked for go into the toilet we filed bankruptcy. The real lesson learned was never to trust the government or the banks and never go into debt.

With our dreams crushed and about the only things left were a 1980 van, our clothes, my old trailer and our family, we decided to move to cactus acres. Somehow we managed to hang on to that property probably because no one else wanted it. By being off grid, no services, bad roads and in an unpopulated area, not a financial institution in America would loan you any money on it, this turned out to be a blessing.

As you have probably figured out by now off grid living is not for everyone. Very few people can really do it or would even attempt it even with today's solar or wind systems which can get expensive it's a whole different life. True off grid living means you only have the power you make and you only have the heat or gas source that you can haul in or is available for delivery i.e. propane, fuel oil or wood. Thermal, hydropower, wind power, and sun power are other sources for heat or electric power. I recently read a story about a family living off grid, in the final ending they admitted to only having to use there on grid system occasionally to supplement their electrical needs, that is not off grid living.

The space age has been catalyst for many of our alternative sources of power used today the problem I see now is that the government has gotten involved. Sure they share a lot of the technology with the private sector and they do offer tax incentives for their use so the private sector has jumped on the bandwagon. With all the new energy companies today, most within the last ten years, the cost has became prohibitive when compared to the return on your investment. This is especially true for the middle class to poor America and a lot of systems are designed to be used with on grid systems.

When we moved to Cactus Acres on a permanent basis, my two oldest sons were married and on their own, only my youngest son moved with us. It was late March and what we had gotten used to calling early spring in eastern Colorado was hard winter at Cactus Acres, we got introduced real fast to a high mountain living.

First off the pond still had about three feet of ice on it and the temperature at night was five to thirty degrees below zero. We had replaced our batteries with new ones but these too had frozen and been rendered useless the only source of power was our old generator. The only way we could get it started was to get it warm which meant keeping it by the fire inside all night, even then there was no guarantee and don't even think about starting your vehicle till late morning or afternoon and then only if the sun was shining.

One story that comes to mind happened around the middle of March. During the night the wind had come up, we had installed a 60,000 BTU heater that ran on propane. It was located in our living dining and kitchen area the bedrooms were on either end. We couldn't get propane delivery because of our roads, location and lack of families living in the area so we had to haul our own using one hundred pound propane bottles.

A one hundred pound propane tank when full contains about 23.8 gallons of propane. Propane produces about 90,000 BTU per gallon or calculating should yield about 2,142,000 BTU's per tank. But these figures depend upon the temperature of the tanks. The lower the temperature the less use you will get out of a bottle. For example, at -20°F you'll only get about half the heat out of those 90,000 BTUs per gallon. What I really am trying to tell you with all that information is we were only getting about three days per one hundred pound propane bottle and they cost approximately sixty dollars to fill.

When we got up about 5:00 A.M. we could easily see our breath, when I went to get out of bed I couldn't move the blankets because they were frozen to the trailer wall. You could see every nail screw or bolt that was in the ceiling on the walls or around the windows as they were white with frost there was no doubt that changes had to be made.

At that time there were four permanent households living here we made it five if we lasted. It doesn't take long to become close as a neighborhood under these conditions we really needed help and guidance. We could get our water from the development well, as every water pipe in the trailer house had long frozen and broke. Two of our neighbors worked in Buena Vista so they could ferry generator gas and groceries when we asked. Remember there were no phones or communication of any kind so you either walked or drove to their house with their help we survived until spring, which at this altitude we found out is around late April or middle May. By spring my son and I had gotten jobs in Buena Vista the pay wasn't much but our expenses consisted of food, gasoline and propane, lots of propane!

The first order of business was to build a house one that was well insulated and we would be comfortable and warm in. We also needed a good insulated shed to keep the generator in and get our 12volt battery system up and running. That's a lot of work for three to four months of summer and would take way more funds then we had coming in.

One of our neighbors told us about a property owner in the development that wanted the old Freeze ranch torn down it had a house, barn and large garage on it. The garage had been used as a sales office when Rawhide Realty was still selling properties and was in pretty good shape. The owner would give us five hundred dollars and we got all the lumber, I thought I had hit the lottery not only was I getting paid I would have the lumber to build our house, what a gift!

The house had been built in the 1870s and 1880s all the wood was native rough cut full dimension lumber. That means a two by four was actually two inches thick and four inches wide not one and three quarter inches thick by three and three quarters wide as is today's lumber dimensions. We got one inch by fifteen inch wide lumber off the siding all made by horse driven saws. There was two inch by six inch and two inch by ten inch dimension lumber and quite a few large support beams. I'm not sure when anyone last lived in the house but judging from the size and amount of the pack rats I'm sure it had been quite a few decades. The first week was spent trying to get rid of rats and the smell we got a lot of the rats but the smell was pretty bad, by wearing masks we were able to tolerate it. It took us about a month to get the house and barn down; one of our neighbors wanted the garage so we gave it to them.

We had half a bucket full of square nails and had found some treasures in the walls. Both the inside and outside walls were one inch by six inch to one inch by fifteen inch lumber which made for a large amount of lumber. Between the walls, as was the trend then, newspaper was used for insulation and because the papers were out of the weather and little dust most were in good condition. I wish I could tell you that we still have them but when you're broke you sell and we did, no we didn't get nearly what I'm sure they were worth today but it sure helped to build our home.

With the old cement mixer my son, wife and I began to make our foundation. First we dug the footers by hand, installed the rebar (metal rod put in concrete to strengthen it) and started pouring it took us about three or four weeks as my son and I both had jobs. With the footings done it was time to build by late September we had our cabin roughed in but far from being ready for winter.

When we could or had the money we would go to flea markets usually in Denver as it was the largest or to auctions to buy windows, doors, insulation, or anything that was needed to build. It was on one of these flea market trips that we found a wood stove it was called a Franklin and was large and really heavy about four hundred pounds. I dickered with the seller and by 3:00 P.M. I guess he figured he was going to have to take it back home with him as on our way out I stopped and offered him $50.00 for it, he took it. With the help of about everyone still at the market we loaded it and left for home.

This was another interesting trip. After loading the Franklin stove and almost everything we had brought to sell into my old '59' Dodge trailer we headed home pulling it with the old '80' Dodge van. About halfway up Turkey Creek Canyon in pretty heavy traffic that we had backed up for quite a distance the State Patrol stopped us. They had their guns drawn and ordered us to get out one at a time and put our hands on the car. After searching us, not telling us why they asked us if they could search our vehicle I figured why not? After opening the side door and rear door and removing the tarp from the trailer they asked why we were going to the dump this late in the evening.

They had stopped us for weaving I explained all I was trying to do was pull over to the right when I could to let traffic pass, I think all they really wanted to do was clear traffic as when the traffic cleared they wished me good luck and let us go. To this day I don't know what the gun thing was about.

Roughed in means you have a frame up with sheathing on the outside walls and roof, we had to wait before we had enough money to buy the tarpaper and roofing. We managed to get the tarpaper on between snows and cold weather to keep out the snow and wind.

That fall my youngest son moved out and got his own place in Hartsel, Jan and I were left to finish building our cabin. By this time what with going through our blizzard experience, building our home in Holyoke and building the large building for our business, Jan had become quite a good carpenter in her own right.

By the winter of 87 – 88 I had managed to get two more batteries, insulate the trailer a little better and torn out all the walls and hallway to let the heat get to the larger area. I had also installed a 12volt fan above the heater to help circulate the air. I didn't do anything to the water system as we were going to try to finish our cabin and didn't want to waste money. I did take two clear storage totes, put a PVC pipe on one end with a shutoff valve and made a shelf above the shower and kitchen sink. All we had to do was heat water on the stove or heater and pour it into the tote to take a shower and rinse dishes; we were still getting water from the public well.

On nicer days that winter we would work on our cabin I had a lot of wiring to do with three separate systems it takes a lot of wiring. The 12volt DC system is wired through a fuse box just like your car. The inverter system is 110volt AC and wired through an electric breaker system like your home. The generator also had a direct connection to the 110volt AC circuits.

I still had to install all the propane lines, we wanted two propane wall lights, a stove, three infrared heaters, a refrigerator/freezer, clothes dryer and a water heater.

The water lines all had to be installed with the central drain so when or if we wanted to leave in the winter on a trip all you would have to do is open this drain and disconnect the pump. This would drain the entire system so it couldn't freeze, remember I said I had designed the system now you know why it took a while.

# **Chapter 16**

The cold nights and early mornings were the hardest. The old 80 van on many mornings wouldn't start and on days that I had to go to work I would wake up three or four times during the night and start the van and let it warm up so I didn't miss any work. Because work is very scarce in the little mountain towns in the off-tourist season, if you weren't dependable they would find somebody that was and I really needed to work.

By the end of December, I knew I needed a shelter to get my van out of the cold. One of my sons was working for a tent company in Denver and could get old drop curtains they would throw away I had him save them until I could pick them up.

I had met quite a few people that had purchased property nearby and had helped them out when asked so I was able to get quite a few two to four inch aspen trees and build a garage frame. Covering the tree frame with canvas curtains didn't look too great but I could start a propane heater in it around 3:00 A.M. and the old van would start. I also put the old Ag Tec generator in it and that sure saved on the back not having to get it in and out of the trailer.

Our biggest expense living there was propane, gasoline, vehicle tires and repairs. It seems I always had a flat tire or needed shocks or new chains. We managed and although I couldn't call Jan if I couldn't get back home from work, I had comfort knowing she could walk to a neighbor to get help if needed. Jan wouldn't know if I was stranded or not and that always caused a lot of anxiety on her part. I always tried to keep forty gallons of potable water on hand in five gallon containers and we had water for the toilet, dogs, and cleaning that we could get from the discharge side of the dam. She was able to manage quite well for a week or so but with no radio, TV or any other communication, it sure did get boring.

I had made a transfer system for our propane bottles so all we had to do when one was about empty was to turn on the valve of the full one and turn off the valve of the empty one. I had five bottles in this system and in the winter you could tell how much was in the tanks buy the frost mark on them. I could haul two at a time in the van so almost always had three full bottles unless it was between paydays then it got dicey. That winter we hadn't gotten a lot of snow and I had only been unable to get to work once. On that occasion it had been bad everywhere in the area so I didn't get into trouble.

By spring we had changed a lot of our ideas on the cabin not the design but how to better install the water and sewer lines to prevent freeze ups and the exterior insulation. Most of our neighbors had not fared any better than us and four of them had been living here for some time. I figured anything short of R-80 in the floor ceiling and walls was a waste of time. Although most cabins had peaked roofs, I had on various trips up noticed that our trailer and most campers I could see had hardly any snow on them but the cabins with the steep sloped roofs were always drifted on the downwind side. I had also noticed when watching newsreels of Alaskan or Antarctica expeditions, that most homes or outposts were dome shaped like the Eskimo's igloos I decided to make the roof flat water would run off but more importantly, snow could blow off.

High mountain snow in the winter is pretty fluffy, that's why skiing in Colorado is so popular and we almost always get wind with our snow. In twenty plus years I've only had to scoop snow off our roof once, well maybe a few more.

I decided to build so we could get maximum usage of the winter sun; I installed our windows to get the most sun possible solar passive heat. Because we are in the open, no trees around us, we get maximum sun good wind usage and the views are indescribable, not only do we benefit from the solar passive heat but looking west up Cals Draw, we are greeted by a tree lined ridge with Mount Princeton (a Fourteener) peak of the Collegiate Range rising high to the heavens. Every day it has a different look you can watch the sun start at its peak and follow it to the house. The sunsets are to die for and in summer you can see rain showers way before they get to you. Looking down Badger Creek South you see Cameron Mountain and rising above it is Hunt's Peak, another Fourteener located in the San Juan range and low clouds hang in the low areas of Badger Creek basin in the mornings giving you a colorful view.

By the spring in what most living here had said was a rather mild winter, with money in short supply and a lot of building to do yet I took another job. I went to work at midnight for a twenty-four hour truck stop and went from that job to my old job and got off at 2:00 PM it didn't give me much time to work on our place but did give us a little more money. At these jobs I met quite a lot of people and through that heard of better paying jobs with shorter hours or seasonal jobs giving more time at home it also gave me access to all the auctions in the area.

It was at one of these auctions that a construction company that had remodeled a Wal-Mart store had kept all the insulation and was selling it. It was two inch thermal in four foot by nine foot sheets with foil on both sides. I bid and got it all for three hundred and fifty dollars. What a buy! I now had enough insulation to insulate our cabin with some left over. To get it home as usual I loaded it all in my van and old trailer. It didn't weigh much but by the time I had it all loaded it was about twelve feet high on both vehicles. I had extended the sheets out over the van cab which gave the appearance of a large semi. The good part was I only had fifty miles to haul it and I didn't encounter any low electric lines which was a good thing what with the foil on each side would have lit me up pretty good if I had came in contact with a live overhead line.

We still only had our tarpaper on the sidewalls so I decided to go to a saw mill in Fairplay and get slabs to side it. Slabs are the outer part of the tree that a sawmill cuts off to square the tree they vary in length, thickness and width and are rather inexpensive, only thirty dollars a bunk at that time, the mill to make them easier to move and stack strapped them in large bundles. Most slabs are purchased for firewood but there are still many buildings in the Rockies that have them as siding today.

Using my chain saw and skill saw I trimmed all the slabs to a uniform width although the thickness varied. It took eight bunks of slabs to make enough to side our cabin and all the trimmings gave us quite a large amount of firewood for our Franklin.

By July we had the slab siding on and most of the electrical, gas, and plumbing done on the inside. We went to a construction auction in Jefferson, Colorado where they had a large amount of new and used lumber along with windows, doors, roofing and a lot of hardware. It was a foreclosure property auction and everything had to sell. Not many bidders were there and the bidding was low end making it possible for me to get some pretty good buys. I spent one hundred and forty dollars and it took me six trips with the van and trailer to get it home, with this kind of luck even with very little money I felt I could start the inside. I framed in the walls for rooms, closets, bathroom, kitchen, and so on. They were already laid out and had been plumbed and wired so it was just a matter of framing them.

We had decided to use the best of the rough-cut lumber from the Freeze ranch for use in our living area. By now, from one of our auctions, I had an old craftsman table saw and my kids for Christmas and Father's Day had given me some very good and useful tools. They had also given Jan tools on some of her occasions and she had gotten very good at using them probably better than I as she was more precise and more particular than I was.

We found while cutting wood in the forests some large and knotty aspens that had died but were still standing, trees that are on the ground for two years or more are usually rotten thus making them useless even for firewood. We found ten really good aspens that we debarked and sanded by hand and used them for inside roof supports we finished them to their natural beauty. The lumber from the Freeze ranch we sanded but only enough to leave the old double bladed saw marks but yet show their natural beauty it's very unique and retains a lot of history.

We had in evenings and when time allowed gathered rocks and had a pretty good pile by that fall. We were pretty selective in our gathering as these were to be used to make the rock walls for our Franklin fireplace. We decided to use a freestanding firebox instead of the built-in because during the blizzard of 77 our built-in fireplace gave us no place to cook or heat water or food and most of the heat went up the chimney. A freestanding stove radiates heat from all sides and has an iron top you can cook and heat on and much more heat enters the home without fans that use electricity. The rock walls would take up a corner between the living room and the kitchen and would extend six feet as a half wall to separate the kitchen, dining and living room areas. The rock would act as a heat barrier and at the same time collect heat and help keep the house warmer when the fire would go out. All three rooms are a large open space design separated by the half wall, here again to circulate heat throughout.

We had a lot of building supplies purchased and ready to install but getting them had taken up the spring, summer and fall. Because of this we had done very little work on the cabin. It was during the fall at the truck stop job that I saw an ad in the paper for jobs at Breckenridge ski slope. There were all kinds of openings I told Jan and my son living in Hartsel and together we went to Breckenridge and applied.

# **Chapter 17**

We all got jobs but with different hours, my job was to meet the grocery supply truck at 7:00 AM six days a week off load the groceries onto my snow cat truck and deliver them to the two restaurants on the top of two different mountains and I had to be off the slope before 9:00 AM. At 400 PM I had to go back up and pick up the trash and haul it to the large containers at the base. During the day I was on standby in case any of the restaurants needed extra supplies, I would deliver them using a snowmobile with an attached trailer. It was a good job for me as by now almost everyone in the country either knew of or had been exposed to my loading talents. It's amazing how much you can load an a snow cat with only a six foot by eight foot bed and no laws to restrict you.

Jan's job was to run the base snack shop. It was her responsibility to stock, inventory and to manage the shop. She would start at 8:30 AM and end at 4:30 PM but because of my after hours work she had about two hours to kill. She asked if there was any work that needed to be done during that time and was given the job of a lifetime, cleaning the public toilets. I can't go into any detail but I doubt there is a worse job at a ski slope. Much to her credit she stayed with it till the seasons end.

My son Derryl's job was managing one of the fast food restaurants at the food court on top of one of the mountains he started at 9:00AM and ended at 3:00 PM. He loved it as he was an avid skier and after work he could ski till closing at 4PM. He would ski down to where I was in the snow cat catch a ride back up and so on till my last run.

With a seventy two mile trip each way we had to leave our cabin at 3:00 AM to get to work on time and didn't get home until about 10:30

PM, six days a week. We did make good money but had no time for anything but work through the winter of 89 – 90.

After the ski slope adventure, one that we all agreed would never happen again in our lifetimes we pretty much agreed the only way to make it here was to be self employed. They closed the slopes in March of 90 and it was then that we got back to building our cabin.

We were still using our old generator to charge batteries for 12volt DC power but mostly used propane lights. They were far more dependable and gave off a little heat as well.

I was also looking into solar panels but in the 80s they were not technically developed to the point they are today they were also very expensive for the amount of power they produced.

Batteries were another problem most batteries were made for autos, boats or electric Golf carts, their average life was two to three years with the constant discharging and charging.

About everyone living in our area was doing as we did for power, lights and heat. Although I had a well for water I was in no way ready for running water in our home we hauled most of it from the community well. What we needed most, especially after our last winter experience was our wood stove installed.

The summer of 1990 saw a lot of changes in our home we got the cabin completely insulated all the water lines were wrapped as well as the sewer lines. The biggest and best improvement was a garage for the van and a small space for the generator and my tools. I installed a small wood stove in the garage area so I could work in the winter and would help to start the van on cold mornings.

We had gotten a wood cutting permit from the forest department and also had permission from landowners in our area to cut and clean their forests. We spent most of September, October and November cutting and hauling wood, we had big plans for selling firewood to make a living.

If there is a harder way to make a living I haven't found it yet not only does it wreck your vehicle but it's just plain hard work. One of the most important tools you need is a good chain saw I did have a chain saw but the good part left a lot to be desired, it was an old Remington I had acquired when I was building our home in Holyoke. It had a sixteen inch bar and had come with a small electric chain saw that I had burnt up in the process of building (at the time it was the only saw I had) but the gas saw was still working. First you have to cut down your trees, carry them to your trailer and load them haul them to the ranch, unloaded them, cut them to length, split and stack. When you sell the wood, you loaded it on your trailer, deliver, unloaded and stacked it for your customer, all this while still trying to be competitive with the professional firewood companies that use mostly automated equipment.

They not only could out produce you but at a cost that's about half that of yours and had contracts with the Forest Department that made their wood costs less than a third of ours. I figured Jan and I handled each piece of wood approximately eleven times. After cutting only four or five loads my old Remington was not only not cutting, mostly because I didn't now the proper way to sharpen the chain but would run about ten minutes before quitting and only after pulling on the rope starter and using some not to flattering language and letting it and I cool down would it start. The last time it did that I got it started and found the biggest tree in the valley cut it and just as it started to fall threw the damn thing under it. But we made the commitment and ran an ad in the paper, it ended up we had way more customers than wood and by December had run out.

We were still able to get to some of the private cuts, but had to hand drag or haul the trees hundred to two hundred yards to the trailer. By February we were out of wood and money and the old truck was pretty tired so we used our time doing what we could to the cabin. The one thing that was a plus in the wood cutting business was the exercise, Jan was down to about one hundred twenty pounds and I had went from my usual weight two hundred five pounds to a lean and mean one hundred and seventy-five pounds. That's the same weight I wrestled in high school. I have told Jan we needed to start our own reality show for the fat farm people we not only could charge people to lose weight but we could sell the firewood. By burning wood it was warm and we used only about a third the amount of propane we used before.

Jan and I spent our time relaxing and doing hobbies. We made some really neat things but like all crafts you really can't make a living selling them. They did however get us through the winter and early spring.

# ** Chapter 18 **

When we moved to Paradise on a permanent basis, Jan had canned some veggies and potatoes and we had put up a crock of pickles. We made a trip or two to the truck farms east of Pueblo, Colorado where we could buy cases of vegetables at pretty reasonable prices. They are picked fresh from the fields and are of good to excellent quality this would give us food for the winter. My mom had hundreds of jars so we only had the expense of lids and ingredients.

As a side note, my mom gave us some special quart jars. She said she had gotten them from her grandmother some of them were dated 1858 and every year we open their contents at Thanksgiving, a pretty unique tradition. To keep canned goods at their peak they need be stored at temperatures of forty to sixty degrees I designed and build a cupboard just for this reason.

Home canning needs to be addressed in more detail. Over the years Jan has probably taught over one hundred people the art of home canning. There are two types of home canning methods, pressure and water bath. If you have a www dot machine (Computer) you'll find many companies that sell supplies, instructions, and recipes. On the Internet you can find just about anything you ever wanted to know and probably some you didn't. As I wrote earlier Jan learned from the best hands on person and there are many little things that seem to get left out in today's instructions.

Canning at 9200 feet compared to sea level is quite different. For example pressure time's change it takes longer for water to boil at a high altitude than at lower altitudes and water boils at a lower tempter at high altitudes. That's not important in pressure canning but has an important role in water bath canning. There are charts you can get or are given by some of the county extension agents or canning supply companies, they will address the altitude issues along with the pressure settings and canning times of the products you are canning follow them carefully. You will find that the fresher the meat, vegetables or fruit the better the outcome. When we can we only buy what we can put up in a two day period.

Although many recipes will use salt we never do you can always add salt to taste but adding before canning seems to diminish the fresh taste. Wash and sterilize all your jars before filling always take your finger and run around the top of jars. If you feel any roughness, check to see if the roughness is caused by something adhering to the glass or a chipped jar if you are unable to get a smooth surface do not use it Jan checks her jars when washing and after filling before applying the lid. Any minute chip or impurity adhering to the glass on the rim and you stand a good chance of having jars that doesn't seal properly.

Make sure to use canning jars, old mayonnaise, jelly or jars used for over the counter foods should not be used, we have replaced most of our old canning jars and give a very close inspection on the ones we do use. Today's jars are far better quality than pre-twenties or thirties jars they're not as pretty but better to use.

I would highly recommend taking a class or getting instruction if you've not canned before but once you do you'll have a hard time eating store bought again.

Your canning tools is an investment, take care of them as you would any fine cookware. Jars may be used for years even at today's cost, if you care for them and use them twenty or thirty years it's a very low investment.

For pressure canners buy only the best and at least an eight-quart capacity anything smaller will be outgrown in a few short years. Buy at least two extra seals with your new canner, we were using my mom's old canner until we couldn't get new seals the canner was as good as new but without seals it's just another pot. Depending on the usage a good pressure canner and extra seals should also last twenty to thirty years. The problem you may well encounter is that today's equipment is built to throw away, they accomplish that by changing styles, sizes, shapes, etc. Soon you may find that you are unable to purchase seal gaskets for your canner and you will have an expensive pot in four or five years.

Pressure canning is the best method as you can pressure red meats, turkey, chicken, their broth, potatoes most all vegetables, the water bath method, though much less expensive, is limited. We only water bath tomatoes, pickles, salsa and relish.

Preserving food can also be accomplished using the brine method. We make sauerkraut and pickles using this method, but I'm sure there are others. We make it a policy to only put up what we like and can use in a year.

Being off grid, canning makes sense as it did in the early development of our country. We not only have meats, veggies, etc., they are as safe, if done properly, and healthier than anything you can buy in the stores. A big plus you will have with canned food it is already cooked if you need potatoes just mash them warm them up and serve the same is true with vegetables and meats which makes for a quick meal.

# **Chapter 19**

By the winter of 91-92, we had seen a lot of changes. We had torn down our trailer and now had our cabin although far from being done it was starting to be comfortable.

There were now two propane companies delivering to our area. Propane suppliers are highly regulated by the government a regulation they take full advantage of. In our thirty years of dealing with them I've had some very awakening experiences. When we lived in eastern Colorado we had very little problems and you had quite a few companies to choose from not the case in our area.

First every propane company must inspect your home to make sure it meets Federal requirements. While federal, state and local codes do vary somewhat they're all pretty much the same but the companies seem to have very different perspectives on how to interpret them. I had one company that actually wanted me to dig up my line from tank to the house to make sure it met the requirements. I had the receipts from another company that had installed it, a distance of four hundred and fifty feet and at a cost of one thousand dollars and change but they said their company wouldn't recognize their work. I found another company to do business with but this isn't always an option especially in rural areas.

I had another company tell me I had to paint my propane tank. It was painted silver to reflect light but they said it had to be a tan color. I don't know why to this day but at the time they were the only suppliers that would deliver to our area, so we painted it tan.

I have used the term, "my tank" several times here as most propane suppliers rent tanks to their customers. Their capacities range from one hundred gallons to one thousand gallons and range in rental price from $50.00 a year to $400.00 a year depending on size and company. The trick here is that one company will not fill another company's tank. If you sign their lease agreement you are locked in to that company as your supplier. The real catch is you're also locked into whatever they charge you for their product, unlike large utility companies in metro areas, price is not regulated. They can also charge you a delivery or pick-up fee which in some cases can be hundreds of dollars but most of all it's the price you pay for propane.

I purchased and now own my own tank, by having my own tank I can call all the available suppliers in the area and get the best price. I have gotten propane for $.40 to $1.20 per gallon less than my neighbor, one and one half miles away, from the same company. It apparently is because he is locked into a lease agreement with them and I'm not.

A neighbor had a lease from a company in our area but only lived here during the summer. When they came back in the spring to open their cabin, the propane tank and regulator (you're required to buy your regulator) were gone. When they left the previous fall there was propane in the tank. After about three weeks they found out that the company had picked up their tank and all because of limited usage. He had paid for two hundred and fifty gallons of propane, the regulator and two years rent, but to this day has not been compensated for his loss and the company is still in business although not in our area any longer.

Another neighbor was doing business with a company and had a lease tank. The company wrote to them saying that because there was a lack of customers in the area they were canceling their service. They did and he still has their tank setting on his property and they still get a bill once a year for tank rental which they refuse to pay. It is stories like these that have persuaded nearly everyone here to purchase their own tanks.

This is probably way more than anyone needs to know about propane and propane companies but it does have a lot to do with off grid living, without propane life would be much harder. There are many more stories I could tell and I'm sure anyone that uses propane in a rural area could tell many more. The bottom line is you must do your homework talk to the local residents but most of all no matter what the cost my best advice is buy your own tank.

In the spring of 92 Jan and I got a job running a breakfast/lunch diner at a private campground in the Buena Vista area, it seemed like a great job because we could work together. We would start work around 6:00 AM and leave by 2:00 PM that gave us every afternoon to work on our cabin. We finished getting rid of the trailer home and I was able to use a lot of the components for our cabin.

The inside was still a long way from being user-friendly but with the temporary fireplace and old propane heater it was pretty warm. I got quite a lot of drywall installed, one of the things I did quite differently is that when I put siding on the outside, I not only laid tarpaper over my sub wall, but also heavy plastic. I also placed plastic on the inside walls before putting on my drywall making it a double thermal wall.

Knowing that the campground job would only last the tourist season I was always open for a fall/winter job. The campground also had a stable for horse riding and leased it to an outfitter who gave dude rides in the summer. The term "DUDE" is meant in a respected way in the west, it simply means the person is not experienced, in this case riding horses. He always seemed short of help or at least help with horse knowledge so in the afternoons on occasion I would take out dudes. Some went on one hour rides and some on four hour rides, which we called Sunset rides. I made more on some afternoons in tips than I did cooking. That same fall he needed a place to put about twenty five head or so of his horses between dude season and first big game hunting season. Our place was fenced in so I offered to board them for the three or four weeks. He accepted and brought out his first load the next afternoon.

Fencing out cows and fencing in horses is a totally different issue. All I had was a perimeter fence with a wire gate to close the driveway. I had fenced our place to keep the cows off our dam and away from the buildings, now I was trapping all the horses inside not the sharpest knife in the drawer.

Cows don't run and even when they do it's not very fast so you can herd them. I found out very quickly that horses that had been in a corral for the last four months or so really liked their newfound freedom. The first thing they did was run to the top of the dam and then down the bank to the creek below. Having not been pastured for a few months and having two good creek bottoms full of grass I'm sure made them think they had gone to horse heaven.

Tall grass fresh water and room to run made for a long three weeks and gave me a whole new take on our place. If we were to board or get horses of our own which we really wanted to do we needed to do a lot of work.

# **Chapter 20**

I got to know the owner pretty well. He was an outfitter for guided bear, moose, deer and elk hunts in one of the few Colorado wilderness areas permitted, and in the fall beginning with the first bow season in September and depending on clients could run well into November. He asked if I would camp cook on some of his hunt trips that fall. I didn't know much about camp cooking but knew a lot about off grid living so figured it was about the same. I found out rather quickly they were not although I used a lot of my experience I also learned a lot that I applied to our ranch in later years.

Outfitters are a pretty special type of people and Bob was off the charts when it came to wilderness living. Although not large in stature five foot six and one hundred forty pounds, I have seen him on many occasions out walk, out ride, out think and yes out hunt everyone he has guided or had the opportunity to work with or for him.

Bob was born and raised in Oregon, his father was a lifelong Forest Service employee assigned to the Wallowa Whitman National Forest as part of that job he would spend a large amount of time building trails, patrolling helping in search and rescue efforts and was a formable outdoorsman in his own right. Bob from the time he was old enough to go with his dad, until his dads death was always with him and from that learned survival techniques that is used to this day along with horsemanship, packing, guiding, hunting and most all other outdoor activities. His mother taught school in one of the last one room schools in Oregon for over eight years and after Bob's dad passing she went to Alaska. She taught in three one room schools located in the Goodnews Bay area the last being at Takiketak, a coastal area on the South West side of Alaska on the Pacific Ocean she was the only teacher until recently, when her age (she was in her late 70's) finally dictated her retirement.

Even through Bob as a youth had spent most of his time in the forest with his dad because of his mothers teaching was a well educated man. After his dad passed away Bob started following the Rodeo circuit. He rode broncos and bulls he has never told me how he did but through some of his old friends I found out he did quite well. It was during this phase of his life, during which he had broken almost every bone in his body along with the cuts and bruises that he was introduced to an outfitter in Colorado that wanted to sell his area and license. Not having near enough money to buy it Bob worked or managed the business until paid for. Having been around horses all his life he started a horse trading business. He would get wild mustangs from Arizona or New Mexico and break them and train them to pack and ride. By doing this he acquired some great pack and riding stock and made it possible to start a dude string. Today he has a dude string in Colorado for summer and after hunting season takes them to Arizona where he has a stable and also does dude rides for the winter.

My first pack in was a totally new experience. First I didn't know what a wilderness outfitter was and I didn't know Bob all that well. I found out rather quickly that being an outfitter means he takes his horses and supplies to his registered area, and unloads everything, and I do mean everything. Wilderness areas are the most regulated areas of the national forest system. No motorized machinery that means chain saws, generators etc. are not allowed. Everything you pack in has to be packed out yes, even human waste! You are allowed propane camping gear, lanterns, stoves, heaters, etc. but again they come out when the season is done.

Bob and his two guides had been making base camp for two weeks before the first season I wasn't part of this operation being a dude or first timer. The base camp is an eight to ten hour ride from trailhead. It takes a lot of packhorses to supply a camp for ten to twelve hunters for six days. Horse feed alone takes about three to four trips with twelve packhorses. There are the tents (six of them), food, sleeping gear, tables, chairs, wood box stoves for each tent, wood cook stove complete with water reservoir and oven, and adult personal necessities (toilet bags, camp toilet, and shower supplies including shower tent. Hunters supply their own sleeping bags but the outfitter must supply the pads and or cots. All necessities you need at home to live had to be packed in including cookware, utensils, dishes, axes, tree saws, the list goes on and on.

By now I hope you're getting an idea of the magnitude of this operation as I did, that first Week was a learning experience for me. Living off grid I saw a lot of ways to make camp life easier and how to cut way down on the gear he was bringing in and out. The first thing was the water. His camp was at tree line, that's 12,000 or so feet in altitude, by a small stream. We did not buy anything that had liquid only dry powered products or dehydrated goods, we did pack in meats and other refreshments.

One of the three thousand or so regulations for wilderness camps is that horses cannot be within one hundred yards of a waterway and all the feed has to be certified by the forest service and the horses are not allowed to graze or eat grass on forest service land thus the packing in of feed. It's the Camp Cook's job to take two horses at a time to water morning and night. By the next pack in I had three hundred feet of one inch black plastic tubing with me. The spring we were using came out of the ground about two hundred feet up hill from the camp. I made a small rock dam in the small spring to backup the water I installed a large funnel into the intake line so water would flow into it and put a screen over the intake to keep out trash. I then ran the tubing downhill to the cook tent, inserted a "T" in the line and continued it on down to the picket line where the horses were tethered. I then dug a hole about two feet across and one foot deep and twenty feet long, laid the end of the tubing in the dugout. I had running water in my cook tent and a water tank for the horses. Because the water flows twenty four seven it couldn't freeze and because it's light and flexible it's real easy to pack the tubing in and out.

For drinking water, I had a two gallon pot with a lid that I could fill. I put it on the wood stove let the water boil a while and then poured it into potable water cans I was always ahead by ten gallons or so for the hunters use.

The shower they had packed in was some sort of a store bought camp shower; it required propane bottles and all sorts of stuff to make it work. I brought up a two gallon garden sprayer extended the discharge hose about five feet, attached the spray nozzle to a tree with a rope about six foot high I then put the shower tent around it. I would heat two gallons of water on the stove until it was about right for showering poured it into the two gallon garden sprayer, pumped up the air pressure and we had a shower. You could turn it on and off or adjust the spray on the discharge hose most all hand sprayers are made this way.

The camp cook stove as I mentioned had a two gallon water reservoir built into it so I never wanted for hot water for dishes and hand washing, etc.

It's amazing what a blizzard and living off grid can teach you after a month or so of camp cooking I felt right at home. I made tortillas, bread, pies, and casseroles and my breakfasts were to die for. I have letters from some of the hunters saying that they actually gained weight.

I built a composting toilet, human waste is mostly liquid. I put a screen that would let the liquid through and discharge the solids into a metal container, when the container was one half full I would put it in the camp fire and burn it. It really worked well and I believe he still uses it to this day, Boy! Did that ever save a lot of work and prevent a lot of messes!

I had to give up my camp cook job because I got too old but there is a side of this story I haven't told, during all my weeks at the camp Jan was home alone. It was the first year I had camp cooked and when the hunters would pack out I was able to go back home for two days before the next season and new hunters would come in. It was about a three hour drive from home to trail head but the trips were very nice and wages and tips were very good so it made it all worthwhile.

The fourth group I did my usual routine by now I was making out my own menus for the five or six days of hunting. Bob would give a count and where they were from, I knew from when we had our business and having stayed in almost every state in the U.S. that the type of food people ate varied greatly and part of my job was to make the hunters as comfortable as possible. I would buy the food on his card and meet at trailhead to go in with the hunters. All went as planned until time to pack out seems he had gotten a late group that wanted to hunt the fifth and sixth seasons. That's late in the high country and puts it well into November.

On the third hunt we had snow but only about a foot or two. He said he wanted me to stay in camp until the end of the sixth hunt, that's twenty nine days straight with no way of telling Jan. I asked Bob to call the Park County Sheriff's office and ask if they could go out and give Jan the message, which he said he did. I felt Jan would be okay, I had bought an old Jeep Commander from our neighbor but it wasn't very dependable. Sometimes it would start and sometimes it wouldn't but she knew she could go to a neighbor to get to town or help, with all things in place I settled in for the long stay.

The worst job was keeping firewood cut it all had to be cut by hand using axe and bow saw and keeping four or five wood stoves going takes a lot of wood.

The hunters usually left camp by 5:00 A.M. Breakfast was always served at 4:30 A.M., which gave me the camp until 6:00 P.M. or 7:00 P.M. when they returned. My day was spent fixing their next day's lunch, getting water, baking, cutting wood, getting their hors-d'oeuvres ready for that evening preparing dinner etc. I would start the sleep fires we had small wood stoves in each tent, around 4:00 P.M. the exception was when they got game, the guide and a few hunters would return to process and hang the meat. That's how my twenty nine days were spent. Now to Jan's story.

In the fall of 91, Steve had purchased an old Jeep from one of our neighbors it had been his dad's who owned a ranch in Wyoming. I am not sure of the model but it was like a big station wagon, I had a hard time driving it because the steering wheel was higher than my head but with enough pillows to sit on, I could do all right. We didn't use it much because it seems something was always broken on it.

Just before Steve left on what I thought was his last week of hunting, we had gone to town and gotten groceries, gas and filled the water containers on the way home. As it was with the other weeks he had been gone it got pretty lonely by midweek, but the dogs and the radio were my company. I could only get one Denver station and it was a sports, news and talk station. I could also get three or four other stations in the evening or at night but they were in Spanish. Although I didn't understand or speak Spanish, I was learning by just listening to the stations.

When Steve hadn't come home by Saturday afternoon I figured he had stayed and helped tear down their camp and would be home soon, but with no phone I could only guess. Time passes very slowly when you're waiting.

The falls here are beautiful once or twice a week elk come down to water as do the deer, there is always antelope on one of the hills around us and of course there is always a badger or two playing nearby. Monday came and although it was a beautiful day, Steve still had not returned and I was really worried. I loaded the dogs in the old Jeep loaded some of the empty water containers and hoped it would start. It did much to my relief and surprise so I drove to Bob's ranch. I guess this was my lucky day because his wife was home she also worked, though I was relieved to know the Steve was okay, I learned I had another two weeks or so by myself. I did my shopping and filled my water containers on the way home. The old Jeep ran fine but I remembered what Steve had told me to do so let it run while doing my errands in town, it sounded terrible but so did most of the other vehicles in town so mine fit right in.

I tried starting the old generator several times but I didn't have enough strength to pull the rope starter hard enough to get it started. Without the generator to recharge the batteries they went dead giving me no radio. It was probably a good thing because by the time Steve got home I probably would have only been speaking dog and Spanish.

I like to crochet and since it doesn't require electricity or power this was a good opportunity. We had our propane lights and left them on all night. I also like to read, especially books on the early pioneer women, most all of them were plagued by the same problem I had boredom. I cleaned the house hand washed what I could and still had a lot of time I had to fill.

It was during the second week and I had just gone to bed when the dogs went ballistic. Keyuk's (our wolf malamute mix) hair was straight up as was Hootch's (a brother to Keyuk [Key – ook]). I took the flashlight and shined it through the front door window and was face to face with a huge bear. I turned off the light, ran to the bed and buried myself under the covers I made both dogs get in on either side of me. It was then I realized I didn't even have a gun. I guess perhaps the bear was as frightened as I was for he apparently ran off and the rest of the night was quite uneventful.

Two days later a neighbor came by to see if I was all right I asked him if he could start our old generator. He tried but his back was bad and couldn't pull the rope any better than I could so he didn't get it to start either. Maybe it was a blessing, but the radio noise would have been nice. I was never so happy to see Steve in my life as when he got home. I vowed never again!!

# **CHAPTER 21**

I have learned more about horses and hunting than I could have ever imagined. Bob taught me how to tie a pack on a horse using a single rope, how to balance the load to make it carry easily on the horse, proper weight so you don't overload the animal and in later years I was even doing some guiding. I got good enough at skinning elk and deer that I could just about beat Bob I could go on and on. I had always wanted to guide and board hunters at our ranch and Bob had taught me enough that someday maybe I could actually make a living at outfitting on my own place.

It takes a lot of teamwork to have a safe and successful hunt as camp cook I was responsible for everything in camp. The guides were responsible for finding game, the safety of the hunters, processing the kill, along with setting camp, on occasion moving camp and after the hunt packing to go back down to trail head.

There are hundreds of humorous stories to be told of hunts but one must be told. Years later I could only cook four or five weeks in a season, my son Greg would take vacation time from his job and fill in for me. It was on one of these trips that he and a guide, Bobbie from Texas, had become good friends but were always playing practical jokes on each other.

Bob had green broke a mustang named Little Buck, a name he had come by honestly. On the last day of hunt Bob took all the hunters out and left Greg and Bobbie to pull camp and take the packs to trailhead where they were to meet up with Bob and the hunters. The story goes that Bobbie had packed the nine pack horses but had somehow got mixed up and only left his riding horse and Little Buck to ride out which of course only left Greg to ride Little Buck.

For those that are not familiar with the term a green broke horse means they can be used for packing but must be put in the string as a lead, otherwise they have a tendency to go right when the other horses go left or visa-versa and that's not good especially if there's a tree in the middle. It also means that they have had a saddle on them but should be ridden by an experienced rider or a bronco rider. They are at best very unpredictable and have a great tendency to buck, run, bite, and things that are just plain meant to irritate the rider.

They got a pretty late start down to trail head it is about a six hour ride but with Bobbie in the rear leading five packs and Greg leading with four packs all loaded heavy it was looking more like a seven hour ride or longer. The first mile or so from high camp is a very narrow winding downhill trail with a hundred yard bog to cross at the bottom that's loaded with red willow bushes. Top camp was still in sight when Little Buck started acting up, rearing a little, prancing, side stepping that sort of thing. That got the four packs nervous and sure enough they got tangled up around a tree. All the time Bobbie hollering good advice like "STAY WITH 'EM GREGOR", or "RODEO OUT GREGOR." Greg finally got the whole mess straightened out with the help of Bobbie, and headed back down trail but had lost quite a lot of sun. They got to the bog and Little Buck didn't want any part of it an especially carrying that thing on his back, he bucked a little, did a little sidestepping but mostly just stood in the mud not doing anything. All the while with Bobbie hollering instructions among them was SPUR the stubborn mule. There are a few things you shouldn't do to a shied horse and never do to a half wild mustang and number one is NEVER put the SPUR to them - he did! At a height of about six feet straight up all you could see of Little Buck was his tail tucked between his back legs and his head tucked between his front legs and Greg about ten foot in the air with one hand above his head holding his rifle and the other hand twisted behind his back with a death grip on the packs lead rope. It seems Gregor landed in a red willow about the same position he was in when in the air only with a red willow branch in a place that takes a lot of getting used to before one can walk in a normal fashion again.

When Bob and the hunters got to trailhead Little Buck was there to greet them and not knowing the happenings of the day Bob was more than a little concerned especially seeing a saddle on Little Buck. He immediately headed back up trail to find Bobbie and Greg. They met about three or four miles in and seems Bobbie was still laughing Greg was walking leading his packs and feeling more than a little angry. Bobbie got the last laugh but shows the type of humor that went on all through hunting season. I had my fun also but in a more subtle way like putting a shoestring in the spaghetti or tinfoil in the pancakes that sort of thing.

I kept my camp cook job in the fall but would only work three or four pack-ins. The money was very good and in 1996 I took a horse as part payment.

# **CHAPTER 22 **

We bought a new generator, with this one I took my time and I knew what I really needed, I had twenty plus years of experience to draw from. From the early 70s to the middle 90s technology has advanced so much that now you had a large assortment of solar, wind, and generator technology to draw from. There are now many generators to choose from some good and some not so good. Ag Tec had been bought out by a huge camping manufacture and had changed the name. The Ag Tec generator was fine it was the motor that we had caused all our problems but like most generator companies you now had a choice of motors you could get so I took a long look at that brand along with a few others. Our needs had changed a lot since the old days so I decided to get a little larger wattage unit, a sixty-five hundred watt unit and buy now I also knew to get a true sign wave unit. We settled for a middle of the road unit, not the best and not the worst that met my requirements as price was still a big factor.

Solar panels although expensive work to the point that if you bought enough of them you could keep your batteries charged even using televisions, lights, computers, etc. If you added wind power, it was and is possible you might only need a generator for backup.

I had hooked up our water system and had the biggest 12volt demand pump I could find at an RV parts distributor and installed an RV hot water heater in the crawl space under the cabin.  I had wired the RV pump to a switch to be able to use it independently. I turned on the pump and after about five minutes we had water to the kitchen sink, lavatory, shower and toilet, we actually got emotional the first flush or so. After twenty three years of doing without, we had hot and cold on demand running water. The next step was a washer and dryer! With electric, water, sewer and propane, our cabin was becoming what we had envisioned years ago now we had to go to work on the rest of our property.

We needed more garage space, a storage building, horse shelter, corrals for livestock, cross fencing to keep livestock from our home, dam and out buildings. We had a lot to do but with both of us working we felt we would have the funds.

After our three week experience with Bob's horses I felt priority number one should be corrals then cross fencing and a shelter. I laid out a diagram of our property and started drawing in fences, by the time I had it laid out it took on the effect of a prison and would probably have taken ten miles of wire to have accomplished it. Back to the drawing board, after a few more attempts Jan and I had agreed on a plan. It would fence in our yard and driveway and the dam, but still give access to the stream for the horses along with all the good bottoms. I had at some auctions bought posts and railroad ties and a lot of fencing, now all I had to do was fence it. Digging post holes in the Rockies was about as bad as when Dad and I had tried to dig our septic system. It took me most of the summer but by fall I pretty much had the cross fencing done and ready for Bob.

# **Chapter 23**

Our first tree planting experience came in 1974 and were we ever dumb. The forest service has a program that will give you seedling trees or sell them at a very great discount to property owners with five acres or more. We had contacted them in 1973, but were too late to get into the program. On the application you give your property location. I assumed the forest service people would guide me in the right direction as to what species of trees would be suitable for our altitude and area which they did. I purchased seedling trees that they had recommended and planted them.

In Eastern Colorado the only trees are in towns and around farms for windbreaks. We planted our trees in nice neat rows and at a distance from the house to give us maximum protection from wind and snow. We had purchased an old five hundred gallon fuel tank on one of our auction trips and was on a stand about eight feet high.

I placed it on the hill above our place, highest point on the acreage, built a pump with a gasoline engine to pump water from the pond about two hundred yards uphill to fill it. I ran black plastic one inch line from the tank to the tree rows and installed a drip line to each tree. The whole system had cost about $100.00. That was a lot of money but not only do trees beautify your property they are very important as they break snow and wind and increase the house heating efficiency greatly in the winter. They also greatly increase the property value.

We planted our trees in early spring as that's when the forest experts had said to do. The middle of May here is somewhat different than sixty miles east in Colorado Springs or Pueblo, Colorado as this is when we get some of our biggest snows and the temperature can range from zero

98

to sixty degrees in one day. They were the experts and although I had made mention of our altitude and temperature ranges I was told it had little bearing on planting trees.

I cut through the ice on our pond and pumped my water tank full. I opened the discharge valve and I was watering our new forest. Trouble was two nights later all my plastic lines had frozen along with my water tank. By mid-June I had repaired my broken water lines but by this time all I had in my rows of trees was brown sticks about one foot high they looked a little like Charlie Brown Christmas trees.

It was obvious I couldn't trust the expert guidance of our forest service so I went to the Park County extension agent only to find that Park County didn't have an extension agent. I was, however, referred to the forest service.

I planted about five hundred trees during the next four or five years but no matter where I bought them or in some cases got small aspen and spruce trees from my neighbor's property, they would all die. The trees I got from our area would last for about two years, but eventually die I even brought up trees from dad's farm in Eastern Colorado, I think they died just getting them up here. The statement that I had made to Jan when we were looking at this property (we can always plant trees) was beginning to sound more like a government promise than an actuality.

I don't recall the year but it was in the early 80's that we were working on our place when a middle aged Mexican fellow and his two helpers stopped in and asked if he could dig up some of my aspens. I guess he assumed I owned a lot of land here as it was pretty apparent there wasn't a tree for a least a half a mile from where they were standing and they were on a side hill only a mountain goat could climb.

I explained that I only had this little plot of land and had been trying to grow trees on it for about ten years and hadn't had any success. It turned out that he owned a greenhouse and his specialty was getting aspen trees from the high country and grafting faster growing species to them. The aspens have a much better root system than their cousins the popular but the poplars grow much faster so by combining the two you get a fast growing tree with a good root system. These were to be used by cities, towns, and highway departments for wind breaks.

He explained that South Park and a lot of other treeless areas in Colorado have a very high alkaline base and the only way to grow trees was to change the soil. He pointed to the tree line on the goat Hill and pointed out that if you look at most tree lines you'll notice new or small trees are on the leading edge of the forest line that's because pine needles act to neutralize the alkaline soil. As the pines drop their needles each year, the water and natural erosion pushes the needles down the hill thus making the soil less alkaline giving the seedlings a place where they can grow.

Over subsequent years I have hauled in many truckloads of pine needles. I have placed ads in the local papers for people to call me when they rake their yards in the fall; I pick up their leaves and needles and mix them with horse manure and some of my soil. I then let the piles set for a year and work it into the areas where I want to plant, I now have trees.

Some of the early planted aspens and spruce trees are now twenty feet high and the aspens are now cloning or spreading into groves I owe it all to that old Mexican fellow who just happened to stop by looking for trees.

It's nice to plant your own forest, first of all you can arrange the trees for best wind protection secondly for appearance and thirdly you can control your views. We have planted trees and shrubs in locations around our pond and yard. The plantings are not only for cosmetic reasons but shrubs and bushes create a habitat for birds and bugs, bugs are a good source of food for the fish in our pond.

In the early days when we had no trees or shrubs we had very few birds so while cutting wood I would get gnarly looking trees and plant them around our area and the pond. These trees brought in birds and helped to make the place at least look like someone lived here. I also bought old plastic Christmas trees at yard sales, auctions and flea markets, it didn't matter what shape they were in but they had to be green. I call this my petroleum forest and unless you get close they look like real trees. More importantly I put them next to my small-planted trees providing a windbreak and holding the snow during the winter. This provides much needed water and additional nutrients when the snow melts and helps to stimulate growth.

We still have about as many petroleum trees as real ones and today we have hundreds of birds including eagles (they like our fish), we get many species of hawks, hundreds of bluebirds, now resident, Canadian geese, many species of ducks and other water and migratory birds. Our place is like an oasis in the middle of a barren land but close enough to heavy forest to get most species of birds and yes many small animals. We see bobcats, badgers, muskrats, beavers, coyotes, rabbits, ermine, and pack rats, some are not as welcome as others but it's with pride that we even see or have them now.

# **Chapter 24**

My son Greg went into his own business and really needed my help. He had bought a catering truck that went from business to business and cooked fast food on their breaks and lunches they are better known as Roach Coaches.

It meant going back to Denver for a while but Jan wanted to go on to school and become a nurse, a lifelong dream. We made the move, rented a place to stay and settled in. We were making trips every weekend and any extra time off. Jan's nursing school was taking a lot of her time so I made a lot of trips by myself. But with a good truck and a big trailer, I had built a thirty two foot long tandem trailer, and a newer three quarter ton pickup truck, and with contacts I made through working on the Roach Coach, I was accumulating a lot of building materials at Cactus Acres.

One of the accounts we fed was a window manufacturer that had hundreds of windows that for various reasons couldn't be sold to their distributors. They kept them in a storage trailer and when full took them to the dump they would let me pick the ones I wanted. I got all the windows to replace the ones in the cabin and quite a few extra for future expansion. All had a very high rated RH factor and most were tinted, or ultra violet rated.

We had our perimeter fence and no fishing signs posted, but by the end of the summer most of our fish were gone. On occasion we would find signs of trespassing, cigarette butts, beer cans, nets, bobbers, fishing line and an occasional dead fish floating. Some of the losses were natural but I've not seen any bears or eagles smoking or drinking beer lately and we do neither as the saying goes "if you build it they will come."

We had a horse to take care of although with plenty of grass and a year round source of water, there wasn't much to do except providing medication and farrier service occasionally. There was of course also the need to build a good shelter and working corrals. Not only did we have our one horse but from late summer to the start of hunting season we had most of Bob's horses as well the count would vary from five up to twenty eight head.

We had cross-fenced our property so our focus was now centered on getting a shelter and the corral done. The shelter only took Jan and me about two weeks to build and turned out really well. I laid it out on the side of our small hill and used pylons for the footers. One of our neighbors had quite a few standing dead pole pines and we worked out a trade for the good straight trees I was able to make all my supports. I decided a thirty by twenty foot shelter would accommodate enough horses for all our needs and any future needs as well. We framed it in and used metal on the roof and inserted a clear panel for light, we had gone to the saw mill and bought slabs for the siding. I should mention that I went to a ranch auction a few years prior and bought about ten tons of strong barn tin. A lot of it had never been used I remember paying sixty-five dollars for all of it; one of the few times I got a good buy.

Our shelter would house approximately fifteen to twenty horses although most of the time in the very cold months of December through March we had only our horse and as years went by it became our horses. We had gotten a colt from one of Bob's horses and had given it to us we had also gotten two miniatures.

It was now time to build our corral, Bob had given us some very good advice on where to best place it and the size. It needed to be big enough to accommodate all the horses but still be able to sort or separate them. It also had to be veterinary friendly, meaning a vet could work on an animal and not get killed by the others.

I wanted a breaking post, that's a post strong enough to hold a wild horse. It may not sound like much, but as an example years earlier Bob had left us two horses and the tack for us to go riding if we wanted. At the time about the only thing I had available to tie to was my five hundred gallon water tank. I tied him up to it and proceeded to put the saddle on about halfway done the Mustang came undone. By the time it was all over the tank still about half full of water was on the ground about two hundred foot from the stand and the horse was so tangled up in the mess that I had to cut the lead rope to get him free up, no it didn't even put a scratch on that old Mustang but it sure bent the hell out of my stand and to this day the tank has the dent in its side.

That should give you a good idea of the importance of a good solid breaking post. It took the better part of two years to get our corral done - twice. I put the corral in its respective area and put in all the necessary dividers and of course my breaking post. When Bob brought his horses and had them unloaded he tied them to the corral rails so he could vaccinate them for the upcoming hunting season. About the second or third horse he vaccinated it reared up causing most of the rest to follow suit. The end result was a corral scattered over about three acres and only three or four corral posts still left in the ground. I spent the better part of the following year rebuilding the corral only this time I dug the posts in three feet deep and spaced them three foot apart instead of the eight foot as on the first one, it's still there.

# **Chapter 25**

Jan had finished her schooling and was working at a nursing home in the Sub-Acute Center, a special care unit, which she thoroughly enjoyed. By the time my job had ended with Greg she had been there long enough to get a transfer to one of the companies' facilities in Salida.

There are two routes from Cactus Acres to Salida, Colorado. The shortest, twenty eight miles via Whitehorn to Ute pass to Salida. At its best, it's bad and if lucky it may get graded once a year. The other route is to Buena Vista and south to Salida a fifty two mile trip one way from our ranch but unless there's a real bad snow is usually always open.

After living in paradise it was very difficult to live in the city or exist in the city as one, in my humble opinion, really doesn't really live in a city. Jan took the transfer along with a cut in pay and we moved back to paradise vowing never to move again.

I answered an ad in the local paper a local hotel needed a maintenance person. They were going to remodel their hotel and needed someone with building knowledge that would work for a very little amount of money. It sounded like the job for me; I had a lot of building experience and had never made much money. It worked out well as they would let me work my hours so Jan and I could share rides.

By this time our boys had all found their own way in life and with little exception wanted nothing to do with our property. They liked to come for a week's hunting season or every so often to fish the pond but only short visits. While we had a nice bunkhouse to stay in we had no cell phone service, computer service, or other on grid conveniences. All we had to do was start the generator to provide those things and I think the boys were okay with it, but the wives and for the most part the grandchildren didn't want to have anything to do with it.

We had the cabin very livable a shop, four-car garage, a horse shelter, fenced in and gated the coral in and quite a few trees growing. Our water system still was working very well and we had two or three propane companies available in our area, life was good. Now it was time to get our solar, wind system upgraded.

With the three types of electric systems I had originally wired into our house, the 12volt batteries had reduced the usage of the generator by about half the run time. By now the wind turbines and solar panels had been developed to be much more user friendly and the term Going Green was just starting to be used. I'm not sure what it meant but seemed to have a good ring to it.

In 1997 we bought our first wind turbine there were four or five companies manufacturing them and a wealth of books on how to build your own check it out on your www dot machine under wind chargers. The one we purchased would produce a maximum output of 500 watts in a twenty six mph wind. The wind turbine must be placed on a tower, they recommended it be high enough to eliminate ground turbulence, meaning above any obstruction that would interrupt the wind current such as trees, buildings, UFOs, giraffes etc.

Dad had an old sixty foot television antenna that I had acquired and brought to Cactus Acres. My original intent was to try to get a television station as there were two micro towers within forty air miles from our property but you need line of sight to get a signal. I had also acquired it to put up a yagi antenna and try to get a cell signal. They had just come out with the Bag Phones, I still have it. I figured if I could get the antenna high enough and pointed south I could get a signal from Hunt's Peak in the San Juan Range where there was a cell tower.

After buying the bag phone signing a contract, buying a yagi antenna, a special built antenna made to receive a marginal signal from a long range, purchasing eighty feet of special antenna wire, several special connections, hanging on top of the sixty foot tower adjusting the antenna while Jan kept trying the phone down below until we got a signal. It must have been just the right conditions because we only made two or three phone calls and it never worked again.

The TV antenna I had installed did allow us to receive two Denver stations but it was kind of like looking through a snow storm to see them, one was the public TV channel and the other a network station. We were more than happy because now we could get the news on occasion and enjoy an evening program. After not having a phone, radio, television or any of the modern amenities for a few years it doesn't take much to make you appreciative and happy.

When I received my wind charger, it was just that the wind charger with no wiring, mounting brackets and of course, it was missing two or three bolts and nuts. After designing a mounting system that I could adapt to the top of the antenna mast (a feat which required three or four trips up and down the mast) and removing the yagi system, I was ready to install our turbine. The wind turbine only weighs about twenty pounds, but my mounting system weighs another ten pounds. It had to be built so the turbine could rotate three hundred sixty degrees still have a good electrical connection and be structurally sound.

It doesn't seem too difficult to climb a one foot wide triangular antenna mast but for a six-foot tall man weighing two hundred twenty five pounds it becomes a rather frightening adventure. My upper body had to be higher than the antenna mast to lift thirty pounds of turbine with a ten foot blade high enough to slip the two and one quarter inch mount pipe into my bearing assembly. I could only hope the rocks on the ground were new as I had heard that new rocks are softer than old ones when you land on them.

I got myself tied in at the top of the mast with the pull rope I had attached to the wind turbine started pulling it up. With the rest stops every so often I got it up to me and tied to the mast. I must've looked like King Kong swatting airplanes because by the time I had it ready to lift over my head and put into place I had quite a crowd stopped on the road above us with their binoculars out watching, I got it into place and attached to the elect lead wires. It took about two and one half hours of standing on the top of that shaky mast and when I got down my legs were so weak they started shaking. I doubt that I could do any of that now although I do still climb up to service it once a year.

The older model wind turbines like mine were rather crude. To keep the turbine from flying apart in high winds they used a system that would tilt the head and blade assembly up. The manufacturer claims that an eighty mph wind would make it completely flat or look like a rotor on a helicopter, ours has been there many times over the years.

Our turbine came with wooden blades and they only lasted about a year before a big bird flew into them. I didn't see it happen, but the whole antenna mast was shaking when I got home from work. Upon investigation I found bird parts along with propeller parts all around the bottom of the antenna so it was obvious what had occurred. How I managed to climb the antenna in a thirty MPH wind and get what was left of the blades stopped without getting killed is another story within itself.

The new blades cost about as much as the whole turbine and I installed them standing sixty feet in the air leaning out from the top of the mast. I will do a whole section on wind, water turbines, solar power, generators and inverters at the conclusion of this chapter.

With the power input from the 12volt wind turbine the batteries seem to stay charged longer before I needed to use the generator charger system. With the addition of the wind charger we had also purchased our first inverter. It was only a six hundred watt unit but would run the television, radio, lights and a 12volt circulating fan. I will also get into inverters later. One important note is that you must know the wattage or voltage of every electric device you're planning to use. For example a sixty watt light bulb obviously requires sixty watts of power. Television sets vary but most use between three hundred and eight hundred watts. You can calculate the power in watts by multiplying the current in amperes by the voltage. My hand drill requires 8.5 amps, multiplying the 8.5 amps times 110volt tells me that my drill requires 935 watts of electric power. You may want to keep this formula for future planning (AMPS TIMES VOLTS EQUALS WATTS). These are just some of the issues that are involved in off grid living, but they are very important in designing and building your system or in designing a supplement system for your on grid emergency system.

Needless to say our six hundred watt inverter didn't provide the needed power for many appliances but we could watch TV if we didn't use other electrical devices at the same time. This is why my demand water pump works so well it's powered by 12 volt DC and not in any way connected to the 110 volt AC system.

# **Chapter 26**

I find it interesting that when we tell people we live off grid almost immediately they think of a bearded gray haired old man with his toothless wife living in a log cabin and eating fish, roots and berries, that image appears to come from some of the survival shows on television. In my wood cutting days I did have a full beard although not gray yet and I'm sure that I looked and met today's frame of mind.

I would like to share an experience with you that happened on one occasion. Jan and I were leaving to deliver a load of wood to a customer. It was late fall and two men in a four wheel drive vehicle flagged us down about one mile from home. They were looking for the location of Badger Creek where the water comes to the surface. When I told him of the location and how to get there, one of the men made a comment I'll never forget. He said, "We hear there are hermits living in this area. Is this true"?

My answer was "Mister you're looking at one"!

We never saw them again but it does show the way most people think of people living in rather remote areas and or off grid.

Many people today when they learn of our style of living immediately want to build an Earth ship or live in a yurt. One lady bent my ear for about an hour on how she and her husband wanted to build a house in the side of a hill and how it would be totally self-sustaining. The usage of self sustaining is a somewhat over used term, although we make our own electricity we still need fuel for our backup generator and without propane our comfort style would be greatly diminished.

There are lots of energy efficient ways to build today and most all are pretty good, we have several in our two hundred eighty plus owner subdivision that have used energy saving techniques, one even built using the straw wall design but everyone here is off grid and must employ some type of electric, water, sewer and heating system. I really prefer to look out my windows at the beauty of the area feel the warmth of the sun or enjoy my fire when it's snowing and blowing outside in my seventy five degree home watching a football game while eating my nachos and drinking a beer, but to each his/her own.

In the past fourteen or fifteen years we have made many improvements to our house and out buildings mostly cosmetic. We have installed better windows (all thermal rated) gotten rid of our old slab siding and stuccoed the complete house. We installed a new roof and totally remodeled the inside with hard wood floors, new cabinets high efficiency forty gallon hot water heater, very nice built in propane refrigerator, new bath tub/shower, vanity, linen closet and even a john, a two and one half gallon flush unit. The entry way has a nice closet along with a small high-efficiency freezer a 1.8 amp unit that uses very little electrical power. I've added a very nice storage area for our canned goods and store bought food supplies. We also have a mud entry area and the washer and dryer are both built in.

What hasn't changed is our electrical system, sewer system, water system, propane distribution, the stone fireplace and we still use the old Franklin wood stove although it's about to get changed out for a new much higher efficiency wood burning unit and while on the subject be very carful if considering a pellet type heater, the fuel cost will eat you alive over a period of time do some research. For additional heat we have installed the new infrared heating systems. We now have a 60,000 BTU vent- free heater for our living, dinning and kitchen area, a 15,000 BTU vent-free heater in for our entry mudroom and two bedrooms and a 5,000 BTU vent-free unit in the bathroom. On this point I would like to inject that we purchased our first vent-free heater in 1983 and have used them every since although most experts will tell you they're unsafe we are still alive, just lucky I suppose!

I use a 1.5watt solar panel to keep my one Marine 12 volt battery charged for lights in my shop and two-car garage. I have the same system for my Quonset building where I house my tractor, trucks and another small shop. I even installed a solar panel and battery system in our horse barn and tack shed.

We have redone all the out buildings, except the horse shelter, with the metal siding and metal roofs from all the strong barn tin we bought at the one auction or have stuccoed them to match the house. We may not have the most beautiful place in the world but it's very efficient and comfortable. I hope with normal maintenance we can spend the rest of our years enjoying it.

# **Chapter 27**

Solar and wind technology was going through the roof and still is. The problem now it seems, that anybody that can spell solar is an expert and to add to the confusion our illustrious Uncle Sam started offering tax incentives to go "green" encouraging all to install solar and wind.

If a company hasn't been in business for at least fifteen years don't call them. I have also found a lot of new wind systems are designed to be connected into the electric grid. They call it "rolling back the meter." you will also find that a large part of their sales pitch is that you will get about half the cost of your system back from the government. In 1997 I paid five hundred eighty dollars for my wind turbine and you can find them today the same wattage for about the same amount of money. Today's technology is better but you'll still not find more than a two to five year warranty.

Here's another caution in an off grid home wind turbine, do you want a 12volt, 24volt or a 48volt system? I could go on at great length about the advantages and disadvantages of all of them. If you're making an affordable system I would use the 12volt, although most off grid hybrid systems today are using 24 volt or 48 volt.

If you are buying 110volt AC system to feed direct to the grid, think twice. First is the cost, they range from seven thousand to thirty thousand dollars you need a place to install it and these units are not small. Find out the cost of insulation and the warranty or guarantee which will expire long before it pays for itself, you'll need both. Check with your city and/or county to see if they are even allowed, and do a wind test before you install your unit. If you are in a low wind area it'll never pay for itself and while I'm on the subject if the grid power goes off and there's no wind, it won't do you much good, I can think of a lot of better ways to spend my money that will save you much better savings and be active in case of a power outage. The salesman will use a very beautiful laid out plan based on average wind speed and government incentives that will make you think you are the electric company some even advertise you can reduce or eliminate your electric costs. I may accept the reduce idea but I'm highly skeptical of the elimination part. I have never heard a salesman nor have I seen an advertisement that tells you about the cost of maintenance. A wind turbine is a machine and I've never to this day seen a machine that doesn't require regular maintenance. Unless you can do the repairs yourself, be prepared to pay an exorbitant price for that maintenance.

Recently, a neighbor who has a hybrid system (that's wind, solar, demand generator and an inverter to run a complete home including a deep well pump) had his system go on default. That means there was a problem in the system. Two thousand seven hundred dollars later he had it up and running again. That was the third time in four years that he's had a serious problem, in his case going green takes a lot of money and I don't believe the government allows incentives for maintenance. I can't say it enough do your homework and ask the right questions. I'm not saying not to use wind, remember I had a wind turbine before I had solar panels, I am saying know what you want before you start buying.

I doubt you will ever see wind turbines used in a metropolitan area unless of course technology changes the design and sound. Space is one reason and noise is the other a small turbine like mine in a twenty plus mph wind makes a high pitched noise I can't hear it in the house but I can in most locations outside. It's hard to imagine several hundred of these working in a congested town. I'm sure they would drive most people nuts and let's face it they would only be attractive when decorated for Christmas.

Solar is likely the best power source to be used on both off grid and on grid systems. When installed properly they're not very noticeable there are companies now that are building them into the roofs and walls making them cosmetically attractive and they make no noise. Several years ago I bought a small solar powered calculator I still use it today and that's part of the upside of solar power.

Solar panels come in various sizes and power ratings, I recently bought a book on solar living, it was the ninth edition and current to the mid nineties the largest wattage panel mentioned was sixty watts. Now I see 175watt twenty four volt panels and there are probably larger ones out there. The cost is quite a bit higher than wind generators with a similar output. A 2400watt wind turbine will cost between six thousand and seven thousand dollars. You would need about fourteen 175watt solar panels costing between nine hundred and one thousand dollars each depending upon your shopping skills. Using one thousand dollars as the cost per unit times the fourteen panels it would cost fourteen thousand dollars for the same amount of power or twice the cost of wind.

The advantage of course is that there is little or no maintenance on solar panels unless they are subjected to hail storms you must also remember that a wind turbine must have a tower, and that may cost about what you paid for the turbine therefore making the cost of solar to wind comparable. Solar panels require sunlight limiting them to fair skies during daylight hours, on the other hand you can get wind anytime of the day or night even and especially during stormy weather clearly there are advantages and disadvantages to each.

Solar power needs the sun and lots of it have you ever noticed that most solar farms are in the desert? There must be a reason. The most important consideration when considering solar power is the location. Trees, buildings, dinosaurs, etc must not obstruct the location for your solar panels. One of the easiest ways to check to see if you have solar obstruction is to lie on your back with your feet pointed at a stationary point then turn your head at intervals in a one hundred eighty degree arc to the right, to the left and straight up, if you don't see any obstructions, chances are you'll have a good location.

Next find out approximately how many days a year your area has good sun. You can usually get this information from your local weather station. Be careful of the information given by Chambers of commerce as they have a tendency to over rate their area, tourism being a good business these days I know about this first hand being in a ski state. While working at the ski area the Denver stations would report snow in the mountains while we were using snow cats to pull snow onto the runs to make them usable.

If you are living in a snow area beware, when snow covers your solar panels and if you don't or can't clean them they're not much good. A thin layer of snow can nearly render your panels useless more importantly the snow will usually freeze at night so even when the sun does come out if not cleaned it could take a while after the suns out before you will get full benefit from your panels. If they are frozen and if you scrape the snow off you can easily scratch the panels, that's not good!

There are four houses in our area now that have tracking systems if you are living in an area that deals with cold and snow be very careful in considering this expensive system. These systems are designed to follow the sun and they do. The first problem with them is that they use extra power which sort of defeats the purpose for which you are installing them in the first place.

More importantly when the sun is between 10:00 A.M. and 2:00 P.M. the panels are almost flat thus allowing them to catch nearly every snowflake when it's snowing. If it gets cold as it usually does when it snows, towards evening the snow will freeze. That in itself is not good, but five or six inches of snow on a solar panel grid twelve foot by twelve foot have a lot of weight, which can burn up the motors that moves the grid.

There is one more "green" system I'm going to touch on. That's hydropower. I was fortunate enough to have two small streams on our property so I have spent considerable time studying hydro or waterpower. When I first considered using my stream for power I did some reading on the subject but didn't understand all the terms that was used, but with my cowboy technology and having seen water wheels in some streams and knowing that water power had a great impact on the development of our country I saw no reason why a water wheel couldn't run a car alternator to charge my batteries.

With all this vast amount of reasoning I began to construct my first hydro system. First I went to Holyoke and got hold of the grain elevator manager had him get me some one bushel leg cups. Ok I'll translate, a grain elevator is a large structure constructed of concrete or metal. There are thousands of these, mostly in the Midwest, used to store grain and are easily identified by their height, in order to get the grain from the bottom or dump to the top, Texas house, they use a long rubber belt with hard plastic or metal cups attached to it. When the belt rolls over the bottom pulley it files the cups with grain, when it reaches the top pulley it dumps it on to another moving flat belt and takes it to the proper silo for storage.

By now you're probably wandering what the hell a water wheel has to do with a grain elevator. I mounted the grain cups between two four foot in diameter wheels to catch the water that ran into them over the top and by filling the cups full of water it would not only spin the wheel but the weight of the water would give me the power to run my alternator. The idea sounded good to me but it didn't work mostly because I not only didn't have near the flow, or water to make it work, I needed at a very minimum forty gallons a minute with a twenty foot fall, at best I had thirty gallons a minute with a three foot fall.

It became obvious not to mention the cost that I needed to do a lot of research before I would be able to convince Jan that hydro power was the way to go. The best information I found on inexpensive systems comes from what we like to call Third World nations. Many small countries in their rural areas have some very good hydro systems using small streams. There are also quite a few turbines made in this country and Europe.

I wasn't able to use my streams for two reasons. I didn't have enough flow or fall the only two ingredients it takes to make a Hydro system. The requirement is a minimum flow a forty gallons per minute with a minimum fall of twenty feet. I was close I have a thirty two gallon flow but the maximum fall I could achieve from my property line to the property line is fourteen feet. I won't go into detail on Hydropower as it only applies if you have access to a stream on your property but if you do why are you paying for your power? The advantage is you can use a twelve volt turban to charge a battery storage system and using a five thousand watt inverter it would supply your home with most all your power needs depending on how conservative you are and it charges your batteries twenty four hours a day seven days a week at very little cost. You can find all the information to build a Hydro system at your local library or go to the Internet then get busy.

## **Chapter 28**

Generators are almost a necessity in any off grid system. They are the best choice for urban areas but if you are living in condos or apartments I doubt they will be allowed and if you are governed by home owner's covenants or property owner associations you better find out if they're allowed. It's a shame that one of your best survival tools may be outlawed just because some do- gooder doesn't like the noise (though when well maintained they're pretty quiet) or perhaps they don't blend in with their idea of beauty. I could really get on a soapbox on this subject, but I believe the recent national news showing a home displaying an American flag and the Home Owners Association taking them to court for violating their rules says it all.

If you are allowed to have a generator in your area you'll find a large assortment to choose from. There are basically three methods of using a generator to power your home or part of it when the grid fails, on demand, direct hook up and portable. From what I see and hear grid failures seem to happen a lot and because of Elmeneo are predicted to get worse.

You will find prices three hundred dollars to in the thousands and if you decide to use an on demand system, the hookup will add to the cost considerably. On demand means just that when the grid electrical system fails the generator is wired to start after a brief delay. Hospitals, emergency service facilities, and manufacturing companies have had this kind of system for years only on a much larger scale than the typical homeowner would use. This type of system requires quite a lot of maintenance and most are timed to start and check themselves on a regular basis. The home systems use either propane or natural gas usually hooked direct into your lines. Propane is as I have written previously widely used in rural areas. It is very unlikely that you could use propane in a city because of how it has to be stored in pressurized tanks. Most cities, towns, or suburbs have access to natural gas and is the most economical of any fuel source.

Gas or diesel engines are by far the best and have a much longer running life, as a wet fuel it is not nearly as hard on your engine as a dry fuel. A disadvantage, however, is that you have to have a supply of fuel stored for backup and you'll need to fill your unit every so often depending on tank size and running load.

As you can probably see by now, there's a lot you need to know. No matter what type of generator they must never be run inside your house as they produce carbon monoxide gas and could kill you. You must make sure there is an open area outside. They make covers for all models and most of the on demand units have their own enclosures if your generator doesn't come with its own enclosure and you make your own make sure it is very well ventilated as most small generators uses air cooled engines and requires a good air circulating space to stay cool.

The use of the generator is for backup only I mean if you loose your on grid power, you really don't need to power your whole house, just the necessities. Circuits that provide refrigerator, freezer, heater, and a few lights are required. Unnecessary are the five or six television sets, two or three computers, all your curling irons, hair dryers, game boys, stereos, coffee pots, microwave ovens, etc and while on the subject what ever happened to the manual tooth brush. Before purchasing your generator, make a list of what power you really need for the next days or weeks to keep warm, cook, keep your food supply and some lights when needed.

At the conclusion of this book I'm going to list our full electrical system and equipment we have for survival for a thirty day period. I am not a survivalist I believe that if you're not back to normal living within thirty days, the country will be in such disarray it really won't make any difference what you have it wouldn't be enough anyway.

As I've said several times before know what you need and do your homework. In the first few chapters I mentioned 5000 watt to 7000 watt generators. They will run most households but I should clarify that I meant only the necessities not with all the toys. Clearly the smaller the power the unit the less electrical devices you can operate at the same time, but the less fuel it will consume.

For example, a 3500watt generator at half load using gasoline will run approximately ten to eleven hours on a three gallon tank of fuel. A 5500watt unit at half load with a six-gallon tank will run approximately eight to nine hours. The larger the unit and the heavier the load the shorter time it will run on a given amount of fuel so know what you're going to use it for and get a unit with the required power output. To determine that requirement you'll need to know the power requirement for each appliance and the length of time that each will be used.

There are three sources to find the amperage or wattage of an appliance, the instruction manual that came with the appliance, on the back of every electrical appliance there's a plate or stick on label where the information is stamped or call your dealer. Most appliances are shown in amps, this would be a good time to find and remember that equation I gave you, it may take a little footwork but the rewards are worth every minute spent. Keep in mind that if you don't open your refrigerator or freezer doors except for necessary usage, a refrigerator will maintain its temperature for five to six hours before you need to recharge and a freezer if not opened can last almost a full day and these units will recharge in two to three hours, so be conservative and only use the generator when needed.

Another subject that needs to be addressed is the proper storage of your gas or diesel generator. If they are primarily going to be used for emergency backup purposes you need to take precautions with the fuel storage and longevity between their usage. Today's fuels only have a shelf life of three months after that they start to loose their potency. A good fuel stabilizer will be needed to keep the fuel usable while stored. Start your generator at least four times a year, like season changes, and let it run awhile and turn off the gas supply to the engine to kill it, this empties the carburetor of fuel and will save you a lot of problems, this of course only applies to gas engines not diesel.

Further tricks that can help to save energy for example would be that when you're recharging your refrigerator plug in your television or computer for that length of time. These units would draw only a small current and won't affect your fuel consumption and you can get caught up on your local or world events, just use some good old fashioned common sense.

You don't have to wire your generator into your home electrical system. Just get one or two good one hundred foot extension cords make sure they are 12/3 or 10/3gauge rated, some of the less expensive cords could cause a power loss. Run the cords through a door or window and plug your appliance into it. If you get a multi-plug extension cord make sure it's heavy enough to handle the load, your hardware store salesman can lead you in the right direction.

Today most every generator has its own built in breaker system making them safer than your own home electrical system. If you overload their output they open the breaker and quit charging.

If you're going to use your television, computer or any device that requires sensitive electronics to operate, you must make sure your generator puts out a true sine wave sixty cycle electrical current. There are basically three types of electrical current output in todays generators: square wave, modified sine wave and true sine wave. The same is true with inverters so I'll cover both now.

With square wave or modified sine wave, the current is interrupted. If you make a square or circle, but do not connect the ends completely, the current must jump the opening to continue, thus the interruption. In today's sophisticated electronics, that interruption can cause it to short and quit working.

A true sine wave is a circular wave with no space thus causing the current to make a smooth and steady run with no interruptions. Sine wave generators or inverters are more expensive, but well worth the extra dollars.

As you can tell by now, I am pretty much sold on a generator for electrical backup. Two big reasons are cost and convenience, but all is not lost if you are an apartment dweller or condo person. I have discussed solar, battery and inverters, now all you have to do is put them together.

Purchase a good solar panel, 130 watt or so take the wires supplied and attach them to a controller (that's a new term). They are not expensive and all they do is keep your batteries from overcharging and blowing up. From the controller take the positive and negative wires they will be well marked attach the positive wire to the positive terminal on your

12volt marine battery or two 6 volt batteries hooked in series to make a twelve volt output and the negative wire to the negative post on your battery the battery posts also are well marked. Inverters are also marked and the smaller units have there own leads again red to positive on your battery and black to negative.

You should get at least a 600 watt inverter, although today's TV's along with the satellite box or cable box takes a lot more wattage to operate, here again do your home work and know your usage before purchasing your inverter. Remember this application won't run a refrigerator, freezer or any other major appliance but it will run electronics and a light very well. You can run your major appliances from this type of system but it will take two or three solar panels, at least four batteries and nothing less than 2000watt inverter.

Most people wouldn't relish having batteries in their living room me neither. A good place to put your solar panel and batteries would be a small porch.

A good mounting system for your solar panel is PVC pipe, it's not expensive and it's easy to build. I used old camping coolers for my battery storage box. They won't corrode with acid won't leak, and they are insulated which helps keep your battery or batteries from extreme temperature changes. This whole system using a small inverter would probably cost less than twelve hundred dollars and it's portable so if you go to the mountains or beach for two or three days and can take some of your toys with you, a friend uses this system for his camper.

Controllers and inverters are two very important parts of the wind or solar system. And I just briefly touched on controllers but like most all things it's a little more complicated than first mentioned. They control not only the current going into your batteries and distribute the current evenly but also keep your batteries from overcharging.

Depending upon your collection system and the amount of current being put into your batteries the controller must be large enough to compensate this current but not allow it to overcharge. It must also recognize your storage capacity or how many batteries you are charging to keep them stabilized. On a small system they are not too complicated or expensive but on full off grid systems (some using sixty or more storage batteries) they get expensive and must be ganged to accommodate this large amount of power.

A good example of this would be a microwave tower on top of a mountain or in a forest, miles from a grid and there are many. Some of these towers use upwards of eighty panels and a bank of one hundred to a three hundred batteries. There are books available or you can go online and easily get the right controller for your application.

Most all wind turbines today have built in controllers and some even have their own inverters. Here again if installing a hybrid system it's best to have professional help or follow one of the many instruction books out there.

Inverters are a very necessary part of any system unless you use only 12volt DC in your home or cabin but that eliminates a lot of conveniences. Inverters range in output from one hundred watts to five thousand watts or more and there are many brands. I recently searched inverters online and found brands I've never heard of from about every continent.

You may have noticed that I've not used many brand names and the ones I have are not in existence anymore. It's not that I don't have my favorites I do, but that doesn't make them the best or worst. I'm not writing a book of endorsements or advertising only some basic information and things I've found that seemed to be missing in much of the literature I've read. Experience still seems to be the best teacher. You now have my disclaimer now on to inverters.

On most full off grid systems they use at least 4500watt inverters. That amount of power will run a deep well pump and most all-household needs within reason. They have built in chargers and are compatible with on-demand generators.

For less expensive systems you need to (as with generators, wind, solar or hydro systems) know your power requirements. A good 2000watt inverter should run a small microwave, vacuum, television, computer, fan, lights or a small pump. Not all at the same time of course, but here again use some common sense. It's important to remember that you must get only a true sine wave unit especially if you're going to use modern electronics.

A neighbor I'll call him ole' Sparky told me a story. It seems Sparky went to the house got the TV set took it to the garage so the boys could watch their game and drink a little beer plugged it into the 110 volt outlet of his AC/DC welder (we are all off grid here). About twenty minutes later there was a loud pop and a lot of smoke. It seems that the old welder put out a good square wave that caused the TV to blow up. Ole' Sparky's wife still gives him a bad time about that. It's kind of a funny story and except for the name it's completely true.

As with generators, most all inverters have overload protection along with low voltage warning and shutdown. This not only protects all your electronics, but your system as well. With the modern technology of todays off grid components it's pretty easy to install some sort of system that is safe and could save you hundreds of dollars in electrical costs.

If you just used two good 6 volt storage batteries hooked in series to make 12volts, A solar panel or two and a small inverter used for your television and computer alone it would probably pay for itself in very little time and give you a good temporary back up in on grid outages.

# **Chapter 29*

Wiring is another expensive aspect of on grid of off grid application. In a small set up like a condo or apartment or just to use as lights it's not much of a factor but if you are using a wind, solar or Hydro system it becomes a pretty large investment.

12, 24 or 48volt DC systems require pretty large wiring. The minimum wire size would be eight gauge but most dealers will recommend a six or four gauge as the leads from your wind turbine to your controller. For those who don't know the smaller the gauge number, the larger the wire. Your automotive jumper cables, for example, are most likely six gauge, the leads on an arc welder are four gauge.

DC power unlike AC power loses power in the wire. The longer the wire, the more the power loss therefore you need a larger wire size to compensate, if you're wind turbine is one hundred feet from your batteries you would need not under six gauge copper wire and I'm sure a dealer would recommend four gauge. It takes two leads a positive and negative plus a copper line for ground. The ground can be twelve or ten gauge AC type solid wire. Just to get from the wind turban to the controller is no small investment.

The mast must also be grounded, which takes a ground rod and some hardware to attach the ground wire. Your dealer or manufacturing company usually has diagrams that you can follow. Although there is a national electric code, every state and county can legally adapt its own code as long as it isn't less restrictive than the standard universal code. It may be to your best interest to go to your county building department and get a copy of their electric codes. Your local hardware store is usually a good source of information and most carry everything needed to hook up your turbine.

Solar panels don't require nearly as much wire or as large as wind turbines and most all panels come with pretty long leads. There are solar kits available now that come with wiring, controllers, inverters and even 12volt lights and a car battery charger. These panels however are usually only 15watt units and come three or four panels to the kit.

If there are three in the kit and it will be advertised as a 45watt unit. If there are four panels it will be advertised as a 60watt unit. My personal feeling is that they are a waste of money as most cost from three hundred to four hundred dollars for a 60watt unit. You'll have four panels one controller, wiring, 200watt inverter and a bunch of special plugs most of which you'll throw away.

A 60watt unit won't charge much and a 200watt inverter if lucky will run a small television or maybe a laptop computer charger. It would take two 60watt units to equal one 120 watt panel. Combined you have eight, 15watt panels and each 15watt panel is as large as one 120watt panel. I guess if you have a lot of roof area or a big yard and you want to impress your neighbors with all your solar panels the kits are the way to go. On the other hand if you want to get the most for your buck you better look hard at a large panel, a small controller and the wiring to go from your one panel to your batteries.

It probably doesn't conform to code anywhere in the United States but I found that an extension cord (twelve gauge) works best for this application. Extension cords are made from braided copper wire and that works great for DC current. They also have the advantage of having the positive, negative and ground built in and they're weatherproof.

The cost of two 60watt kits will cost approximately seven hundred dollars. The cost of one 120 watt panel, one small to medium-size controller and the wiring will run about eight to nine hundred dollars As I have said many times, do some research and shopping. I may not be right on target but it should give you some good places to start applications to think about, ideas about the right questions to ask and the hidden costs only found if lucky in the very small print. With today's copper prices, wiring is a big expense and so are certified electrical contractors.

If necessity breeds intelligence, with all the mistakes I have made in developing our ranch and the intelligence gained from them, must make me the smartest person in America.

# **Chapter 30**

Over the years we've had some very humorous and not so humorous experiences. Most come from new friends, visitors or curious new property owners in our subdivision. We had some friends stay one year for about a week. They had been to our place before but only in passing through we had been to their home many times. It was late fall, but the pond wasn't frozen yet although it did get chilly at night. On the second evening the wife confided in Jan about how surprised she was we had lights, television, computer, running hot and cold water and even the tub and shower. After quite a lengthy explanation from Jan on how we had most all the amenities in our home except a dishwasher, she asked Jan how we flushed our toilet. Jan took her into the bathroom she showed her the little chrome handle on the toilet tank and explained that she had to push it down. True story! It's an example of how many people have a total misconception about off grid living.

Our phone system is a microwave system. There's a tower on a high hill and the company puts a pole in your yard or somewhere on your property with a solar panel, battery, a control box, an antenna and the lead in wire to your home. The only requirement is that somewhere on your property you must have direct line of sight to the tower from the antenna on your pole.

Our acreage happens to be only approximately a thousand yards or so from the tower with no obstructions but there are owners here that have had to buy an adjoining lot or have a forty-foot high pole to accomplish this line of sight this makes for a pretty expensive phone, but better than none, as was the case before 1998. Our private phone company may be the best in the country (I just had to brag a little).

Now they even provide high-speed Internet service which is not in any way connected to your phone system. They use the same pole but larger battery and solar panel and extra equipment. They have no contract and no equipment or hook up charge and so far we've experienced no service interruptions. Now you know why I bragged on them not bad for wilderness living.

My youngest brother and his family from the East Coast came to our place only once in the thirty nine years we've owned here and then only for two nights about twenty years ago. Our place was in the rough then and they weren't impressed except perhaps by the fact that they did catch the rainbow trout from our pond and got to cook and eat them the same day. I have no idea if they even remember the experience, but I do.

We have had several family members here (both sides) but only once or maybe twice. Jan's brother after years of asking finally came from Denver he rode his big Honda motorcycle to get here. I don't think he was impressed with the twenty two miles of rocky dirt road from Highway 9 outside Hartsel and wasn't here two hours when he saw a cloudbank building in the west, he was back on his cycle and gone never to come back. I could go on and on, but there are friends that not only love it here but a few have even bought here and built, some actually envy our lifestyle.

Is not hard for a man to adjust especially if they like the outdoors but it's a very hard life for a wife, homemaker or professional to adapt. Even today, most women that have built here with their husbands won't live here full time.

I don't believe it's the area (God knows it's peaceful and beautiful), rather it's the lack of accessibility to the urban lifestyle. Just to go to the hair stylist in winter takes a lot of planning and then they may have to cancel due to weather, shopping or going to visit friends in another town takes some planning and in some cases washing, cooking, house cleaning, washing dishes and a lot of just common chores takes some special getting used to. Others have freezers full of food and enough supplies to last two or three years, but only come up two to six times a year and then usually for a night or two. There are six or ten ladies like Jan that love it so much that going shopping even in the small town is an outing that's done only out of necessity. It's not necessarily a hard life it's just not a convenient life especially in this pushbutton world.

The most wonderful part of living here is the people. We all have a common fondness for off grid living or we wouldn't be here. Therefore when we on occasion all get together it's a real hoot. We have people from all walks of life from preachers to professors from paupers to millionaires but you'd never know it on hoedown day it is definitely days of old, brought back.

Most all the people that have built and live here have their own lifestyles. Their electrical, water, and sewer systems are similar and yet very different. That doesn't make them good or bad, it's just that if it works for them, then it's good. I like my system and I'm very proud of it, but there are much better ones and some not quite as good.

Our electrical system is pretty simple. The porch, entry, overhead bathroom, and both bedroom lights are all wired 12volt DC. The dining room, kitchen, living room lights and all lamps are 110volt AC using the inverter. The outlets in the living room are all on the inverter. In the kitchen, half are inverter and the one in the hallway is on the inverter. The other outlets are generator direct, two in the kitchen, one in the living room, one in the dining area, one in the bathroom and one in the hall. With a transfer switch I can put all inverter circuits into the generator direct and bypass the inverter. My reasoning for the direct generator outlets is they are in areas where we use heavy drawing appliances microwave, garbage disposal, washer, dryer, toaster and other high energy applications. Our inverter would probably carry most of these but the draw on our batteries would require recharging them by using the generator and battery charger so why not just use the generator in the first place.

Most RV's have an electrical diagram that comes with the unit. If you can find one it really doesn't make any difference what kind or year as long as it's made before 1975 follow the main wiring diagram to the breaker system that's very similar to my system.

Our water system is no different from your home only that my pump is a 12volt on demand from a direct source. If you're on a well it will save you a lot of money and headache to pump into a holding tank or cistern. They make many sizes and shapes and its not hard to make your own, I would recommend nothing less than a six hundred gallon tank depending on your location and room to install it. It makes little difference where it's located in your home many here use their crawlspace as you can run a line from the pump to any cold water line to hook it up. Most RV 12volt demand pumps will carry about forty five pounds of pressure and they make some that will pump seventy five pounds but if you install a 110volt AC pump you can adjust your pressure. Keep in mind that if you're off grid a 110volt pump requires quite a lot of power to operate.

The sewer or drain system is no different than any other home. Just follow your state or local codes. It doesn't matter whether you're on a city system are a septic system. Septic systems require some special care I put a yeast product in mine every thirty days or so and have it pumped every two years. I don't really know if it's necessary but I've had few freeze ups or leach problems since its installation in 1972, so why change?

# **Chapter 31**

I promised some tips on short-term survival gear to keep in your home in case of bad storms, electrical outages that sort of thing. There are many booklets out there that address this very subject. A good place to start is your local emergency center. I will tell you what we keep on hand and after going through the '77' blizzard and my wilderness cooking experience we have never been without our E. Kit. Keep in mind this emergency kit is for power outages gas failure or other disasters in your home, it is not meant for living in a tent or other areas away from your home as you need the food, cloths, tools and other products of home living to bring it all together.

A small propane stove the type that uses one pound disposable throw away propane bottles is essential. They will last about three hours and if used sparingly can give you even more usage. There are several types available, a good source is your hardware store or sporting goods store. We have a two burner type and they cost approximately forty dollars. There are adapters available to convert it to accept larger propane tanks also. I am not fond of using your barbeque as a cooking source or a heat source they discharge a lot of carbon monoxide so must be used outside and in our blizzard it was covered with twenty foot of snow anyway. A LP heater is essential if you're in a cold or marginal climate. A four thousand to nine thousand BTU propane type works well if used in only one room but keep a window or door cracked as it must be ventilated these are readily available at most hardware stores or camping outlets and will run about three to six hours on a one pound bottle and forty eight to one hundred hours on a twenty pound tank like your barbeque uses. This type of heater will keep a two hundred square foot area pretty comfortable and are used widely in tents, fishing huts, small cabins, campers, etc; They cost in the eighty dollar range, there are larger units available but bear in mind the larger the heater the more propane it will use. In addition to these, five or ten gallons of potable drinking water in good water containers, a camping lantern, and two flashlights with extra batteries are also desirable. We also keep about six extra one pound disposable propane bottles on hand. As you have read I am also a big believer in generators for emergency back up purposes, even a thirty five hundred watt unit can supply power for small appliances and your refrigerator if used one at a time. I recently got a brochure that had a thirty five hundred watt gas unit for two hundred eighty dollars, it didn't indicate whether it was a true sign wave or not. With heat and water and being in your home you should be able to survive well for quite some time.

It's my sincere hope that among all my dumb mistakes and learning the hard way that you take away something useful. I've gone into detail on some points that I felt were very important and I'm sure I've left out some but I feel that if you follow my advice it will or can save you a lot of expense and still give you a good serviceable system, either for off grid or on grid applications.

Although we live off grid and have given some advice on our development and systems, there is a lot of information on how to apply it to on grid situations. It can save one quite a lot of money and at the same time make life very tolerable in power outages or other unexpected disasters. Most people will spend more on eating out or other entertainment in a year than the cost of most of my survival material and never give thought to a disaster. The time to fix the fence is before the cows gets out.

The most important message I hope the reader understands is for you the users. Do you really need to have half the lights on in your home? Why not only use them if you need them? Try doing some hobbies or play games or God help you read as a family using one light.

Do you really have to leave your two, three, four or more TVs on all day? For that matter do you really need that many TVs? Do you have to leave your computers on when you're not using them? I know your reasons but maybe it's worth the extra ten minutes it takes to boot them up, computers uses a lot of power even when on rest.

The last time I was at a friends home and we were going out to eat, as we were leaving I walked through their home. I counted eleven lights on, two television sets that were hooked to game boys one computer all on and the heater thermostat set at seventy five degrees. I didn't say anything as I'm already seen as an extremist, but on several occasions I've been told what a rough time they're having making ends meet.

I watch in homes when visiting people and they're leaving their faucets on to rinse dishes while all the time they are washing them in the sink not using the running water. Filling the dish washer a quarter to half full just wastes water and can add up to big expenses, dishwashers are one of the largest water and power wastes in a home.

People flush their toilets after each use sometimes they simply throw a tissue into them and flush each pull of the handle uses from three to five gallons of water. I understand the sanitary issues but for hundreds of years the old outhouse was used, and in national forest parks and roadside rest stops still are and other than an occasional spider bite I haven't heard of anyone dying from using them. Maybe every other flush would be ok. It's no wonder our water resources are disappearing.

I recently bought a new kitchen stove we have to use gas and most all the new gas stoves have automatic strikers that use electricity. I found only one manufacturer that doesn't use the glow plug for the ignition system in their ovens. In researching the glow plug system I found it takes one thousand eight hundred watts to two thousand watts of electric power to operate them and they call them "energy-efficient". Two thousand watts is the equivalent of having twenty; one hundred watt incandescent light bulbs on at the same time in your home.

I'm sure the old pilot light ignition system was unsafe by today's pushbutton standards, but furnaces, water heaters, and gas cook stoves were using them from the early 1900s until about five years ago, now they're unsafe - don't figure.

There are television commercials, books, papers, and so on telling you how to go green. I really get a kick out of those funny looking light bulbs they're pushing now. First is the cost at eight to ten dollars each, you could use a ninety eight cent incandescent 60watt bulb quite a few years before the new bulbs would pay for them selves. I can maybe see their savings in a commercial setting where light is needed all day , but for home use why not just turn off your lights when you leave a room in the first place?

The term "green" is used from cars to homes, books, glass, plastic, clothes, toilet paper well you get the idea, personally I like the word "conserve".

If you get a chance to drive in the country look closely at the abandoned homes or shacks as they are known. Someone built them and lived there probably with the same vision Jan and I had but for unknown reasons left. One can only imagine the dreams hard work and disappointments that they must have endured. I find it amusing and sad at the same time when I see photos on calendars, in the history books, postcards, and paintings and occasionally on television of old cabins, ranches, ghost towns, etc. People buy these pictures and hang them in their homes, offices etc; or they watch documentaries about them because most people deep inside have a desire to live in that time, truth be told however most people today would starve to death or die of dehydration if there were no grocery stores or they lost their water or electric supply.

While developing and building our dream it was not possible financially to live here and most all of my young to middle adult life was spent working to raise my family and make a payday to payday living but Jan and I had a dream and to accomplish it we never put ourselves in a situation that would jeopardize that dream and by our late middle age was able to live it and still are. If living this type of life style is thought of as backwoods, why then on most week ends and holidays is there a mass exodus out of the city to areas like ours?

Give some thought as to how fragile life is and what you can do to conserve or save our resources. This earth is billions of years old and it will probably be another billion or so older before all is done but human life is but a speck of this timeline. That speck is already depleting earth's ability to sustain life as we know it, a little help from all of us would go a long way toward preserving resources for future generations.

As Jan and I get older and our health deteriorates there is no doubt we won't be able to live here much longer. We can't afford to hire people to do the necessary maintenance. If we can't drive how do we get to doctors, stores, etc? These are just a few of the many problems age brings and being in the country adds to them. I have no doubt that when we do move we will be on grid but our electric, water, and gas bills will be much lower than the average Americans because we don't know how to live any other way.

As a last footnote, this spring we had a junk man come and clean up our ranch. I gave him all the iron for payment which included the old '59' Dodge trailer. You guessed it about a month ago while in Salida we saw someone pulling it and was loaded high and tight. I believe it needs to be put in the Smithsonian.

*Picture of Our Ranch*

LaVergne, TN USA
14 November 2010
204850LV00001B/215/P